WOMENTREPRENEURS

WOMENTREPRENEURS
Inspiring Stories of Success

Avinash Kirpal

SAGE

Response
Business Books

www.sagepublications.com
Los Angeles • London • New Delhi • Singapore • Washington DC

First published in 2016 by

SAGE Response
B1/I-1 Mohan Cooperative Industrial Area
Mathura Road, New Delhi 110 044, India

SAGE Publications Inc
2455 Teller Road
Thousand Oaks, California 91320, USA

SAGE Publications Ltd
1 Oliver's Yard, 55 City Road
London EC1Y 1SP, United Kingdom

SAGE Publications Asia-Pacific Pte Ltd
3 Church Street
#10-04 Samsung Hub
Singapore 049483

Published by Vivek Mehra for SAGE Publications India Pvt Ltd, typeset in 11.5/14.5 ITC Century by Zaza Eunice, Hosur, India and printed at Chaman Enterprises, New Delhi.

Library of Congress Cataloging-in-Publication Data Available

ISBN: 978-93-515-0554-9 (PB)

The SAGE Team: Sachin Sharma, Sandhya Gola and Ritu Chopra

To the passionately committed young girls whose life mission is to improve the quality of life in marginalized communities by overcoming sociocultural challenges.

Bulk Sales

SAGE India offers special discounts
for purchase of books in bulk.
We also make available special imprints
and excerpts from our books on demand.

For orders and enquiries, write to us at

Marketing Department
SAGE Publications India Pvt Ltd
B1/I-1, Mohan Cooperative Industrial Area
Mathura Road, Post Bag 7
New Delhi 110044, India

E-mail us at **marketing@sagepub.in**

Get to know more about SAGE

Be invited to SAGE events, get on our mailing list.
Write today to **marketing@sagepub.in**

This book is also available as an e-book.

Contents

Foreword

G irls in India have been encouraged by traditional families to take up professions such as teaching or medicine. They have also been taught that they should focus on home and family. This is despite the fact that many Indian women have taken remarkable initiatives for the upliftment of society and made a deep impact both at personal and societal levels. The names of Kamaladevi Chattopadhyaya and Durgabai Deshmukh, among others, easily come to one's mind.

The perception about the roles of women in society has now dramatically changed. Women have reached great heights in diverse professions and vocations, as pilots, astronauts, engineers, academicians and bankers, and in public life.

The entrepreneurs featured in this book have used different criteria for measuring the success of their undertakings. Interestingly, most of them have not emphasized profitability. For them, the most important concern is the social upliftment of different sections of society and of course issues of environment.

This book presents the work of women entrepreneurs across a wide spectrum and in various fields. For instance, Binalakshmi Nepram from Manipur was stirred to action by seeing many innocent women and their families devastated on account of the gun culture prevalent in Manipur. Urvashi Butalia is a doyenne of feminist publishing, bringing to light issues concerning marginalized women. Also, there are other women who have been tirelessly working, for example, in creating awareness in coping with children afflicted with autism (Merry Barua) or in ameliorating the problems faced by destitute unmarried mothers (Lakshmi Krishnan). There are also other women who have achieved remarkable success in providing consultancy in human relations, in the hospitality industry and in creating employment opportunities for rural women.

These experiences can guide young aspirants who are concerned about striking a balance between their careers and their family lives.

Avinash Kirpal and SAGE Publications deserve credit for taking the initiative to produce this inspirational work at a time when the economic scenario as well as the socio-cultural environment in India are set to support the efforts by young women who have the courage and determination to accomplish noble entrepreneurial work.

Kapila Vatsyayan
Chairperson, Asia Project
India International Centre

Acknowledgements

I would like to acknowledge with gratitude the support and encouragement received from many individuals who have helped me directly or indirectly in the completion of this book.

Saroja Khanna

My friend Saroja's livelihood had been from publishing and journalism, as well as from telling stories to entertain little children. She not only provided feedback that helped me to clarify my thoughts at various stages of the book's preparation but also enhanced my capabilities to acquire fresh insights into entrepreneurial behaviour by taking me (often dragging me!) to performances, book launches and meetings with bureaucrats, diplomats, business people and academicians, which broadened my perspectives and enriched my writing.

Since a manuscript has to pass through various computer systems, a writer is expected to be conversant with the popular computer languages as well as requirements such as downloading, formatting, filing and so on, at all of which I am absolutely hopeless. Saroja helped me sail through this maze of electronic wizardry so that I could get together a reasonably professional-looking document.

Himadri Das

I am indebted to my erstwhile colleague Professor Himadri
Das, Director at the Great Lakes Institute of Management,
Gurgaon, and formerly Professor of Finance at the
International Management Institute, New Delhi, for his
guidance regarding the selection of people who could par-
ticipate in my project, some of whom he had taught at
business schools. I also thank him for his advice about
how to deal with problems associated with the emotional
and psychological needs of female entrepreneurial aspirants which, as a teacher, he understood very well.

Himadri also explained to me ways of asking probing
questions so that during interviews one could uncover
hidden truths. This substantially enhanced the depth of
the stories in the book.

Patricia Orrico

I am grateful to Patricia Orrico, Director, International
Federation of Industries, Salvador, Brazil, for inviting me
to visit Salvador and for providing me with international
perspectives and viewpoints on the subject of entrepreneurial projects. She introduced me to several successful
Brazilian women entrepreneurs who told me about the
sociocultural challenges that they faced and who responded
actively, in a question and answer session, to information
about what their counterparts in India had to overcome.

Sachin Sharma

Sachin Sharma was the specialist deputed by SAGE
Publications to help me write a manuscript of acceptable

quality. In spite of my very frustrating and annoying ignorance about publishing practices, Sachin meticulously and patiently persevered with tutoring me and made this project come alive. He never hesitated to provide a helping hand, enabling me cross the rough patches that inevitably appear in such journeys. I am very grateful to Sachin for being so considerate. Without his encouraging attitude, I would have not been able to develop capabilities to write inspirational stories and I would have remained a lesser writer.

Introduction

Businesses and philanthropic ventures established by women have contributed significantly in many developing countries by enhancing welfare and employment as well as by increasing the variety of goods available for the local market and export. Apart from these measurable benefits, a greater involvement of women entrepreneurs in the economy has other advantages: because of their natural predispositions, women are sensitive to issues concerning the environment, avoidance of waste as well as promoting ethical and decent conduct; these serve to civilize society as well as encourage sustainable development.

This book tells the stories of 10 women from various backgrounds and from different parts of India who started entrepreneurial businesses or philanthropic enterprises after overcoming major sociocultural challenges. For example, it is often mentioned that our society, which is dominated by men, expects women to focus on family and home and that such an expectation makes it difficult for female entrepreneurs to perform tasks that are necessary for establishing projects, such as travelling and meeting people. Other challenges include the tendency among men in the business world to not accept women as fully committed to their start-ups, and in fact to regard them as promoters who would soon quit in order to take care of home issues. When financiers, suppliers, customers and prospective employees think like this, it becomes very difficult for women entrepreneurs to create enterprises.

The stories illustrate how opportunities for women entrepreneurs are changing because of globalization and new technologies as well as the liberal social ideologies sweeping across the world and across India. The stories show that the motivations for women starting entrepreneurial ventures no longer arise predominantly from the need to supplement income but increasingly from fulfilling a need for creative expression and individual growth as well as a desire to benefit society. These developments, together with the spread of education amongst girls, have created a new breed of modern Indian women entrepreneurs and also shifted the focus of their enterprises from home-oriented products to products and services that are based on knowledge and technology, as well as to humanitarian and developmental activities.

Some of these women had the benefit of business education, others had some formal education, whereas some did not have any education at all. The stories of MBAs who started businesses include diverse areas such as trading, hospitality, executive search and HR consultancy. The stories of women who established humanitarian NGOs include areas such as care for adolescent unwed mothers and their children, care for people with autism and their guardians, the welfare of nomadic tribes, sustainable development and ecotourism.

The book also considers the lessons that emerge from the stories as well as ideas concerning issues that are frequently faced by female entrepreneurs. It looks at the personality traits of the entrepreneurs while investigating the causes of their success. It also highlights some of the common mistakes made by women in the course of creating and running their ventures: for example, their tendency to try to manage too many activities single-handedly resulting in stress. Some entrepreneurs do understand that a solution is to delegate to knowledgeable professionals but, as shown in some stories, the hiring of professionals is itself a problem because they tend to avoid entrepreneurial start-ups headed by women. The stories show some novel ways used by the women entrepreneurs to overcome these and similar challenges.

The stories are based on material collected through personal interviews. The book uses the format of 'stories' rather than of 'case studies' to engage non-academic readers. The stories have been selected not because their projects were outstandingly successful in terms of growth or impact but because they demonstrated imaginative ways in which sociocultural challenges and prejudices were overcome.

1

Shailja Dutt

Talent Search

Building strong relationships based on mutual support and good faith is a dominant feature of Shailja's style of doing business. She always had an almost childish belief that if you do a good deed to help another person then your action will, in some magical and mysterious way, eventually rebound and result in something good for you. She invested considerable effort in developing relationships by finding ways to help people attain their aspirations. Shailja also loved to dance. As she learnt salsa, tango and cha-cha-cha, she reflected on the similarities between dance and business. 'Both are about passion and being nimble,' she thought; and later as she ran her business, she had this in mind.

When Shailja was planning to establish Stellar Search in 1998, she had some upbeat ideas about the kind of company she would create: she would employ bright management graduates who could interact comfortably with the senior executives of top-of-the-line corporate clients and she would have a well-appointed office equipped with modern communication infrastructure from which 'Stellar' would conduct an international executive search business. But there were a few hitches. First, she had no money. Moreover, it was unlikely that any bright young management graduate would join her start-up at a time when established well-paying companies were offering secure jobs; office accommodation was hard to find and office equipment was expensive; top-of-the-line clients would hesitate to try out a new search firm for key appointments. So it seemed it would not be easy for her to create her dream company.

Now, in 2016, Stellar Search has come a long way and is recognized as a premier provider of executive search services to leading Indian and foreign MNCs. It has arranged over a thousand senior management placements across diverse industries, functional areas and geographical locations. Stellar does business in India as well as in Dubai, Singapore, Malaysia, the Philippines, Thailand, South Africa and China. Its clients include leading names like Nike, Adidas, Shell, Maruti, Bausch & Lomb, Johnson & Johnson and Gillette as well as companies belonging to the Tata, Essar, Birla, Mahindra and ITC groups. More than 60 per cent of Stellar's business comes from existing clients—a testimonial to performance. It employs more than 40 people and has an annual revenue of around ₹10 crores. Within two years, Shailja plans to convert this figure that represents revenues into a figure that represents profits. When that happens, Stellar would have a valuation in the market of about ₹200 crores.

The Formative Years

Shailja comes from a Marwari family, which moved from Rajasthan to Kolkata before independence. (The Marwari background would show up later in her career when her decisions demonstrated that her genetic programming supported business acumen!) She spent her childhood in her grandparents' home. Her grandfather was president of the Calcutta Stock Exchange in the heyday of its glory, but he was also a nationalist, a freedom fighter and a Gandhian—switching easily from suits to khadi kurtas. Her grandmother was from the typical sophisticated *bhadra lok* (bourgeois society) of Kolkata. Shailja's childhood in this environment was happy and full of stimulation. However, in 1971, Shailja's parents decided to leave Kolkata and move to Delhi. The move to Delhi did not result in a happy home. There was domestic strife, and soon her parents separated. Shailja was then brought up by her mother who was only 17 years her senior and a simple school pass-out from Bara Bazar.

Her parents' separation changed Shailja's life in many ways. For example, the family underwent a sudden severe financial crisis, although it had been financially comfortable earlier. In fact, Shailja's mother had to sell her jewellery to look after the expenses of the home and to bring up Shailja and her two sons. Living became extremely frugal. Shailja recalls how she often travelled to college by bus without a ticket and sometimes changed buses to dodge ticket checkers. There was often no money to spend in the canteen, and she avoided the company of friends who frequented restaurants. Living this way also resulted in certain personality traits in her, which would be useful to her later: she became independent, adventurous and street-smart.

From her childhood, Shailja had been keen on becoming a doctor, and it was a great disappointment to her when she could not get admission into a medical college in Delhi. However, with the high marks she obtained on leaving school, she got admission in Lady Sri Ram College for Women in the University of Delhi and studied economics.

Shailja did not enjoy studying economics. It did not seem an appropriate subject for someone who had dreamt of becoming a doctor. In college, she was considered strange because of her lackadaisical attitude towards studies. While students tried to occupy the first rows in the classroom, Shailja was content to be in the last row, where she quietly read novels. While other students were immersed in books and lectures and their minds were full of plans about CAT and IIMs, Shailja spent time reading novels in the college gardens. It was only when the exams came near that she took some interest in her studies. Much to everyone's surprise, including her own, Shailja did exceedingly well in the exams and got a first division. In fact, throughout her student days, both in school and in college, in final examinations, she had always been amongst the top few in her class.

After attaining her degree, she put together some savings and bought a cheap ticket to the UK. This trip was mainly intended to check out the status of a romance with a childhood sweetheart who was then studying in London. When she arrived in London, she discovered that the magic had evaporated. However, she stayed on in the UK for a year travelling, doing odd jobs and experiencing life. There was a hue and cry about this in family circles in India, and serious doubts were expressed about whether such conduct would enable her ever to get a suitable husband. But Shailja had decided and done what she considered was right for her.

Shailja returned to India in 1992 and realized that she needed to build a career. She decided to get some work experience and worked as a consultant with the Strategic Management Group and with the McKinsey Knowledge Center. While working as a consultant, Shailja joined the part-time Post Graduate Diploma in Management program at the International Management Institute (IMI), New Delhi. This is a grueling course designed for working executives who wish to obtain management education and qualifications without giving up their jobs. They work during the day and study during the night—for three years. It requires hard work and dedication. About what she had learnt at IMI, Shailja says: 'The most useful learning came from interactions with peers, including persons from different backgrounds and from various parts of India, with different experiences and aspirations.' At IMI, she got deeply interested in studies.

Apart from the knowledge she gained at IMI, she also got herself a husband. Shailja married her class fellow Sunir Dutt during the third year of the course at IMI. She had always been among the toppers in class, whereas he had generally been close to the bottom. She helped Sunir quite a bit with studies. In fact, she ended up doing homework assignments for two students. (Later in life, Sunir's unfailing faith in her entrepreneurial abilities would be a source of great emotional and moral support to her business venture.)

Launching Her Business

After completing the course at IMI in 1993, Shailja contacted Amrop, the leading worldwide executive search firm, which was then commencing business in India to take advantage of the liberalization in the economy. A strange thing happened when she met with the Amrop management: Instead of finding a job for her, they offered her a position within Amrop. She readily accepted this offer because she felt that she had a flair for spotting talent and that her personality suited this field. Shailja worked with Amrop for three and a half years and enjoyed her work immensely. She learnt a lot and rose in the organization quickly. She started as an associate and soon became a consulting partner. However, after a time, she became restless and felt the need for a change. She took a few months off to introspect about future plans. Having seen the executive search business from the inside, she believed that the search process could be improved in many ways. She also foresaw a large market opening in India that could be serviced better by search firms that were not saddled with the rigid regulations of large firms like Amrop.

Shailja had her first baby in 1997. She then wanted to be the master of her own time so that she could spend more time with the child at home. This would be difficult while working with Amrop. Sunir encouraged her to start her own business because he understood that a person like Shailja needed to be out working instead of staying at home. Shailja quit Amrop in 1998 and started her own executive search firm: Stellar Search. By then, she had formulated her ideas about how executive search could be conducted efficiently using the organizational behaviour concepts she had learnt at IMI as well as modern information and communication technology.

Why did Shailja decide to start her own business? She explains: 'I wanted to do the executive search business differently and I wanted it to be my own creation. With us search would be more than placing the right person in the right job, it would be an opportunity to effect positive organizational change and forge lasting relationships. We would be partners and passionately involved in our clients businesses.' With the burgeoning of the executive search industry in the mid-1990s, corporate recruitment in India underwent a paradigm shift towards proactive methods rather than the traditional database/advertisement methods that were already being considered as inefficient. Top-of-the-line clients wanted executive search firms to go out and search out the right people for the job instead of waiting for people (generally second rate) to apply in response to advertisements or to dig out names from databases (again generally second rate). Moreover, the 'with-it' clients sought executive search firms that would work closely with their top management and contribute at the strategic level in addition to contributing at the operating level. It was in this niche space that Shailja wanted to place Stellar. Also, she wanted Stellar to be a specialized boutique search firm and focus only on senior- and top-level searches; she did not want to dilute the brand by getting involved with searches for junior-level managers or management trainees because she considered that a different ball game involving different skills.

Shailja's mission for Stellar was to 'create excellence in management through executive search by identifying outstanding professionals for specific business requirements'. It was a comprehensive mission statement, and Stellar's culture, strategies, style and approach to work were derived from it. Shailja says: 'With our clients, we define organizational needs and design strategies for each search. We work within agreed time frames and costs. We provide the client with a process perspective so they gear up to expectations accordingly. We do not encourage shortcuts.' Stellar assists in the first interview and in subsequent negotiations as well as facilitates the candidate's induction into the company. This support stands behind every engagement, and a time-bound replacement guarantee accompanies every search. Utmost discretion and confidentiality is guaranteed to clients and candidates.

Dealing with Challenges

Establishing and running Stellar Search involved several challenges. An issue that often confronts women entrepreneurs is that people feel that women are not totally committed to their start-ups and would leave soon to devote time to home and family. When financiers, suppliers, customers and other business associates as well as prospective employees think like this, it can make things very difficult. How Shailja dealt with some of the major challenges is discussed next.

The first challenge Shailja addressed was getting a team together. The bright MBAs whom she wanted in her team were sceptical about joining a fledging start-up. Shailja thought up an innovative strategy: She began to teach at business schools, and she used the opportunity to educate students about careers in executive search as well as groom them for such careers. 'I did want bright young MBAs anyway, and this seemed like a good way of getting to them.' Stellar now has a powerful team of educated and trained professionals handpicked and coached by Shailja. There are specialist consultants focusing on different verticals, supporting cross-functional consultants and back-office staff. Shailja herself spearheads all general management and board-level recruitment. She also counsels companies on recruitment strategies and organizational restructuring. Incidentally, whereas many medium-sized firms in the HR services sector employ professionals part time, with only a loose bond with the firm, Stellar employs full-time professionals who are exclusively on the rolls of Stellar.

Shailja's second baby in 2002 was a difficult delivery as one of the expected twins had to be aborted. Shailja was bedridden and distressed; she considered quitting her business, but Sunir persuaded her to carry on. She agreed to get back to work gradually. Stellar, had been losing business because of her prolonged absence, and it was evident that she would need to spend time on organizational development. Shailja encouraged her staff to be involved in social work. This helped raise the motivation, commitment and morale of her employees. Stellar's corporate social responsibility efforts started with the education and vocational training of some of the company's own employees from underprivileged backgrounds and included coaching to improve computer literacy and English language capabilities of Stellar's blue-collared staff as well as of the domestic help of the employees. On a larger canvas, the efforts included quick response to natural disasters—Stellar was one of the first organizations to respond to the Red Cross call to help Tsunami victims. To institutionalize and formalize these philanthropic activities, the Stellar Foundation was created. It provided primary education to children from underprivileged backgrounds. Also, the foundation used Shailja's persuasive powers to obtain contributions from clients to supply items like water purifiers and blankets to needy people and to take on the responsibility of treating any critical illnesses. Stellar's staff spent time on these activities, which contributed to defining the corporate identity of the company and to build a team imbued with the Stellar ideal of doing good to others.

With respect to marketing, Shailja admits that she was naïve in the early years. She presumed that once she made it known that she had started her search firm, clients would come to her because of her well-known record. That did not happen. The very people who had been happy to deal with her when she was in Amrop thought twice before contacting her when she had established her own search company. Later, she developed and implemented a proactive marketing campaign. She personally approached managers who she had placed in senior positions—and who remembered her skills. Slowly, they began to come to her with search requests and then stayed with Stellar as they moved from one company to another. Shailja had always believed in building strong long-term relationships, and this belief played an important part in her personalized marketing campaign. Once, a candidate she had placed in an investment bank lost his job because the bank folded up in a financial meltdown. Shailja helped him to regain his self-confidence by inviting him to sit in her office. While he was in her office, he unwittingly became responsible for introducing a person who later was to become one of Stellar's most significant business contacts.

The services of a modern executive search company are of course more expensive than the services of a traditional employment agency. The former could charge about five months' salary as fee, whereas the latter would charge about one month's salary. Indian clients were used to the rates charged by the traditional employment agencies, and so Shailja had a difficult time changing the valuation of executive search services. Fortunately, the dot.com boom and the liberalization of the economy resulted in many large foreign companies entering India. These companies were aware of the benefits and costs of modern executive search, appreciated the value offered by Stellar and accepted its fee structure.

To differentiate Stellar from competitors, Shailja also emphasized the use of modern information and communication technology. Stellar's knowledge management systems capture data and process information regularly. Shailja says: 'As pioneers in knowledge management for executive search, we use our own proprietary software as well as other programs. We communicate in all sorts of ways. We have an elaborate website and we are in the professional and social networks. We use voice over internet. We skype, we post, we text, we blog and we tweet.'

The involvement with technology enabled Stellar to provide executive search services to clients in other countries. For example, Stellar helps Chinese firms to locate and recruit managers, including local Chinese candidates, and South African firms to locate and recruit managers, including local South African candidates. Using its high-tech back-office facilities in New Delhi, Stellar functions like it is physically present in the foreign countries.

Financing is a perennial problem faced by woman entrepreneurs. When Shailja started her business, she had limited funds. She had to borrow ₹50,000 from her husband to find office space. She finally rented space for a rent of ₹5,000 per month in a basement and started operations from there. She had to buy a computer and stationery on EMIs! She permitted herself the luxury of appointing a secretary mainly because she felt that clients would be more impressed if the telephone was answered by a secretary. In the first year of operations Stellar yielded revenues of ₹24 lakhs, much higher than the expected revenue of about ₹12 lakhs. In the following year, they stood at ₹60 lakhs. She repaid her loan, and soon Stellar had sufficient funds to employ a receptionist and a secretary as well as two people for back-end office work. After that, there was no looking back. A remarkable feature of Stellar's growth has been that Stellar was funded entirely from internal accruals. Shailja never borrowed again and she did not seek equity participation. She planned the expenses for running and growing the company, and the required funds were generated from within the business.

A big issue that many women entrepreneurs in India face is tackling bureaucratic hurdles to obtain the required registrations, licenses and permissions to start a business. A lot of people simply give up because of the hassles. At various fora including the press, electronic media and the Internet, Shailja has advocated efficient and transparent administration to promote entrepreneurship. Further, she says: 'Not enough is done in our schools and colleges to develop in our students the urge to take risks and create businesses. The government focuses too much on a few feminine issues which propagate the stereotype of women as weak victims who need to be protected.'

Personal Matters

Shailja's personality is suited to executive search. She makes friends and influences people easily. A client, a candidate, a service provider or any other business associate is quickly won over by Shailja's earnestness, helpfulness and charm. When interviewing, she can get candidates to relax and open up. When presenting a business proposition to a client, she is persuasive because what comes through is basic integrity. The key words that spring to mind when describing Shailja's style are unconventional and passionate. She is modern in her thinking and behaviour but is also at home with Indian traditions. So we have here a blend of modernity and tradition, which enables her to get on well with both kinds of people. Dominic Mellonie, HR Director at Expedia, Inc. (UK), describes Shailja: 'She is westernized in her approach and massively passionate about what she does.' Her ability to harmonize with different kinds of people helps in opening many doors. She has a strong code of conduct based on personal integrity, fairness, respect and consideration for others. She sees through waffle and hypocrisy.

As Shailja was building Stellar Search, her husband, Sunir, became a senior executive with General Electric. He lived and worked in Guangzhou, China. His contract enabled him to visit Delhi every month and Shailja visited him in China six or seven times a year. They made this arrangement work very well.

Shailja feels that this arrangement enriched their marriage as they spent a lot of quality time together. Their two boys lived with Shailja and studied in Delhi schools. Sunir's parents also lived with Shailja, and her own mother lived nearby. Now Sunir has been transferred from China to Singapore, and Shailja has moved her home from Delhi to Singapore. The operations base of Stellar, however, continues to be in Delhi.

Entrepreneurship literature often mentions that marriage and children make it difficult for women to pursue entrepreneurial careers. However, in the case of Shailja, these factors had the opposite result. Her marriage contributed considerably to her starting and staying with her business. The birth of her children made it difficult for her to be employed by somebody as she needed to be master of her own time. So having her own business was a solution rather than a problem.

Shailja has interesting advice for budding entrepreneurs: 'Have a clear goal and business plan. Keep the long-term objective in mind as you tweak the short-term plans by setting small, achievable, short-term objectives. Prioritize well between board meetings, dentist appointments, sick toddlers, nagging moms-in-law, spouse's boss at home for dinner, etc.; tackle each, one at a time. Be honest; do not compromise for short-term gains. Nurture relationships, respect people and build an emotional bank balance. Keep innovating and changing.'

Shailja believes that the entrepreneurial path is not a bed of roses, but she brushes aside the suggestion that 'no great success is achieved without great sacrifice'. In her opinion, some compromises and a degree of adaptability are required, but these are certainly not 'great sacrifices'.

Shailja is not interested merely in increasing the size of Stellar. To her, success is measured by the quality of services that her company provides. So success for her would include high-profile recruitment as well as the ability to influence corporate strategic decision making. Moreover, there is the charitable work funded from Stellar's income and from donations arranged by it from clients. To Shailja, these represent 'a giving back to society' a part of the gains earned from society and are a significant measures of success for Stellar Search.

2
Merry Barua

Action for Autism

Merry Barua is the founder and president of the National Center for Autism, a pioneering institution that made India a leading country in the region with respect to caring for children with autism, providing succour to their parents and promoting general understanding about this stressful condition. Earlier in the 1980s, Merry had been a journalist and a marketing executive in the corporate world in Kolkata; her infant son had then started to exhibit intense behaviour. This was later diagnosed as autism. At that time, there was very little awareness about autism in India and parents suffered agonies because of the lack of information.

Autism is a brain disorder that becomes noticeable in children as they grow out of infancy. It manifests in extraordinary conduct, particularly with respect to communication and social behaviour. It upsets the way in which the brain processes information and prevents people from properly understanding what they see, hear and sense. A combination of factors can cause autism, including biochemical and hereditary factors as well as structural changes in the brain. There is no medical treatment for autism, although medication may be used to treat specific symptoms. Although autism impairs a child's social and communicative skills, it heightens sensory perception. However, people with autism perceive the world differently, and therefore communicate and react differently. They have to learn ways of communicating and of relating to people, and unless they are taught, they will often use unruly behaviour to express their needs. Researchers believe that a large number of children in India are autistic, although most have not been properly diagnosed or given appropriate guidance, especially those among the rural poor.

Ignorance about Autism in India

Till about 2000, there was very little awareness about autism in India. Very few professional doctors had heard about it, and fewer knew anything about it. People seeking information about autism had few options: one was to find medical books in the American or British libraries in major cities, and for those that did not have access to such libraries, there were not many options left.

In 1980, Merry gave birth to her son Neeraj, and as he grew, he began to exhibit challenging behaviour. For over two years in one hospital after another, doctors misdiagnosed Neeraj's case till finally, in 1984, a lady psychiatrist in Kolkata, Ms Ratna Kumar, examined Neeraj and said that he was autistic. The parents had no idea what that meant and how to deal with it.

In those days, most medical professionals in India confused autism with 'mentally ill', and treatment for autistic children generally involved attending schools for the mentally retarded where the same teaching methods were used for all students without consideration of the fact that autistic children needed to be handled very differently, in fact individually. In the absence of sufficient understanding about autism, appropriate interventions did not happen and autistic children seldom showed improvement.

Coping with a Diagnosis of Autism

The experience of discovering that her son was autistic is described by Merry: 'When Neeraj was just a baby, I was a raw mum with my first experience of motherhood. I noticed when I tried to cuddle him, he pushed me away screaming inconsolably. In his crib, he stared endlessly at the toys rotating overhead. He slept little. So neither did I. He ate little, but mealtimes were stressful; they took forever, and most spoonfuls were spat out. He destroyed most toys, and his favorite activity was throwing anything he could lay his hands on out of the window. One of my earliest memories of Neeraj's strange social behavior was during a visit to a relative; Neeraj was only interested only in the daughter's toy duck, and during the entire visit, he lay on the floor manipulating its moving parts. Then again at a birthday party, he spent two hours lying on the floor pushing a toy truck backwards and forwards oblivious of the activity around him. Neeraj's childhood was chaotic, but I thought then that this is what child rearing was all about—an exhausting but normal experience which every mother has to face. I comforted myself with the thought that with time things would become right. So my emotional anchor then was the hope that the chaotic experiences were temporary and would pass. However, as Neeraj approached the age of six, his behaviour became increasingly intense, and then came the diagnosis of autism from Dr Ratna Kumar, which shattered my hope that this would only be a passing phase. It became evident that the difficulties with Neeraj, the screaming tantrums and distressing scenarios, would not go away. They were there to stay. This was very hard to accept.'

For a parent, a diagnosis of autism is like losing a much-loved child and then welcoming another. We grieve for the child who is now gone. But we must grieve briefly so that we prepare ourselves for the child who has come.

Despite the initial shock of the diagnosis, Merry quickly came to accept her son's autism. But there were other issues too, particularly the 'odd' behaviour that accompanies autism, and Neeraj had more than his share of this behaviour. Since he looked 'normal', it was often a matter of what people thought of the mother. Poor mothering was a common observation that mothers of autistic children had to constantly face in those days; even though scientific research had firmly established that there was no connection between the occurrence of autism and improper parenting. Also, there were factors such as disobedience and non-compliance. Demands placed on individuals with autism seem pointless, leading to unwillingness to comply, and the apparent disobedience shocks onlookers.

Merry's Beliefs and the Quest for Knowledge

At that time, Merry had no strong religious beliefs. Her spiritual strength came from her faith in herself and her belief in the power of the mind. Since childhood she had this trait of not allowing adverse circumstances to make her mentally depressed. She believed that happiness is within one and needs to be reached out to. She also believed that a person had a duty to oneself and to others and should work towards cultivating a positive and optimistic attitude. This belief helped her cope with adversities and also inspired others.

Merry had studied at the Loreto Convent in Kolkata. Mother Teresa had been a nun there and had, as a teacher, given up a comfortable life to work with the poor and the diseased, which made her truly happy and deeply content. Her example had taught Merry that that despite living in a world that worshipped materialism, one could be happy without wealth.

The diagnosis of autism put Merry temporarily into a state of shock and numbed inaction. She remained in this mental stupor for about a month but finally snapped out of it and spurred herself on. She realized that she had to take charge and make things happen. She did the only thing she knew to do when faced with a difficult situation—take action. She began to learn about autism by subscribing to foreign journals and importing books. She also collected information about what was happening in India and in other countries with respect to autism.

In the course of Merry's search for information about autism, her attention was drawn to the work being done at the Nambikkai Nilayam special needs school in the Christian Medical College in Vellore. She was aware that the doctors and faculty there, like everywhere else in the country, were still groping with autism and had no real solutions, but she also noted that they were sincere, dedicated and trying hard to learn. The treatment at Nambikkai involved the mother and the autistic child living together in a tiny apartment and spending a lot of time together so that the mother's natural instincts were utilized in a healing process.

Emphasis on frugal living and egalitarianism was an aspect of the treatment at Nambikkai, which made a deep impression on Merry. All families, rich or poor, were treated equally, except that the poor were charged less. So a rich mother and her autistic child could live next to a poor family. Merry found much wisdom in the Nambikkai culture and took it onboard for use in her own future plans.

In 1985, Merry decided to take Neeraj out of the nursery school in Kolkata and took him to Vellore where mother and son were admitted to Nambikkai.

Merry had intended to spend three months there but she eventually stayed on for six months working intensively with Neeraj. There were noticeable improvements in Neeraj's behaviour. Merry also gained useful knowledge. After mother and son returned to Kolkata in late 1986, Neeraj was put back into his old nursery school and

later into a special school for handicapped children.
However, there was no improvement because the teachers lacked knowledge of autism and sometimes responded
to Neeraj's 'aberrant' behaviour with ineffective punish-
ments to which he reacted violently.

Developing a Strategy

In 1987, Merry's husband was transferred to Delhi and the
Baruas moved out of Kolkata. In Delhi, Merry encouraged
the formation of a group of parents with autistic children.
The group started with three mothers and their autistic
children. To help each other and build social skills in their
children, this miniature support group organized get-
togethers and outings. At the same time, Merry began
writing articles about autism in the popular press. These
articles generated many responses from parents of autistic children appealing for advice and help. After receiving
many such letters from parents, it became evident to
Merry that it was time to address this need by creating a
larger network of families concerned with autism, which
could share ideas, disseminate information and provide
mutual support. So the idea of creating a national organization to support autists and their families began to take
shape. This eventually led to the creation of Action for
Autism (AFA)—a society founded and directed by Merry
to provide support to persons with autism and their parents. AFA, among other things, advocated a way of accept-
ing autistic children for what they were and then helping
them learn and progress, while also creating a social environment that helped people with autism to grow to their
full potential. AFA had its roots in the empowerment of
parents. It was registered as an NGO society in 1991.

Merry's search about how autism was being dealt with in other parts of the world indicated that it would be useful for her to attend a course for the parents of autists being conducted at the Options Institute in Massachusetts, the USA. This intensive 5-day course was very expensive, but Merry decided that it would be worthwhile, and in 1992, she went to the USA with Neeraj. Having invested a lot from her savings, Merry was determined to extract every possible benefit from the course: In the classes, she took copious notes and even purchased a dictaphone to record everything that happened. The course in Massachusetts proved to be a turning point for Merry. It helped clarify her thinking, which had become confused because of the turmoil of the past. Her views about dealing with autism changed considerably. For example, she found relief in receiving reaffirmation that Neeraj's off-putting behaviour was not an intentional rejection but a symptom of his confusion—an issue related to autism that needed to be understood.

However, the course in Massachusetts could not solve the difficulties Merry faced with regard to Neeraj's condition. For some inexplicable reason, Neeraj's behaviour started deteriorating rapidly when Neeraj was in his teens. For a period lasting more than six months, Neeraj experienced a rage, depression and anger that he could not control, which were expressed in exceptionally challenging behaviour. Merry says: 'It was like living with a caged tiger. I dared not take him out of the tiny apartment where we lived then. An apartment that was reduced to a wreck as he tried to find an outlet for his feelings. I tried to help him deal with the emotions raging through him, but with little success.'

Driving Action for Autism

It was at about this time that Merry became convinced that she herself had to do something soon to bring about changes in dealing with autism, so that other mothers did not have to experience the confusion and isolation that she had suffered. She took on a leading role in bringing about changes that would ensure that information and help about autism would be readily available in India. She made strenuous efforts to reach out to others concerned with autism. She used the knowledge and skills from her past experience in advertising and journalism to promote the awareness of autism. She started a journal *Autism Network*, which she wrote and printed herself; she began to counsel as well as run intensive home programmes for parents. She also started a small school in her home in Defence Colony, New Delhi, to help autistic children

Gradually, Neeraj's communication improved and the flashes of intense behaviour became rarer. Soon other children with autism joined Merry's school. This led to the creation of the Open Door School in New Delhi in 1994. This school received national acclaim and became India's leading school specialized in helping children with autism as well as their parents (parents who initially may have regarded their autistic child as a liability but then learnt to enjoy their child).

Some of Merry's outreach efforts were on a small scale while others were on a national, even global, scale. One of the modest efforts included writing a piece dispelling myths about autism and pasting this onto video library cassettes of *The Rain Man* in which Dustin Hoffman plays the role of an autist.

Merry's bigger outreach efforts included growing the activities of AFA and leading it to establish The National Centre for Autism (NCA). This institution brings together persons with autism as well as their parents, professionals and researchers in a single location. Since 2005, the NCA is located in its own four-story building in Jasola, New Delhi. It is a pioneering institution which demonstrates that, unlike in the 1980s, there is now understanding, care and support for autism in India. Merry did laudable hard work for overcoming all the daunting bureaucratic, legal and regulatory hurdles involved in establishing an institution in New Delhi, even if it is philanthropic.

All the services and facilities that Merry and other parents of autistic children in India had sorely missed when they were bringing up autistic children are now available at the NCA. These include diagnostic assessments, counselling, teaching and training. The assessments, which are the starting point of formulating a plan for each child, are conducted through comprehensive observations by clinical psychologists using internationally standardized criteria. Other assessments cover functional skills as well as occupational and sensory traits. Support services include social communication programmes that facilitate the entry of autistic children into mainstream schools as well as cocurricular activities like computer training, pottery and home management that enable autists to become fully participating members of the community. Special programmes for parents include counselling and training, such as the 10-week-long 'Mother and Child Training Program' regularly conducted at NCA by trained therapists for about 20 parents and their children.

Gone are the days when parents had to visit American and British libraries to get information on autism. The NCA is a comprehensive resource centre with India's largest collection of books, journals and materials on autism. It has an elaborate website. Its publications include the monthly *Autism Network*, which focuses on autism in the Indian context and has been appearing regularly for the past 20 years, as well as a variety of guides and training manuals. The Open Door school, which started from humble beginnings in 1994 and then became India's premier institution for teaching autistic children, is part of the NCA. It has become the model school for autism in India. It not only imparts education and training but also conducts research. Like a laboratory, it tests, adapts and modifies teaching and training techniques. Currently, the school has about 70 children aged between 3 and 18 years placed in seven sections according to their needs and abilities. It also supports autistic children studying in other schools. The centre has special intensive programmes for outstation families so that they can benefit from counselling with NCA's educators, therapists and psychologists. The centre reaches out to over a thousand beneficiaries each year. Merry is now trying to expand the facilities at the NCA to include temporary accommodation for outstation visitors.

At the NCA, autism is not regarded as a tragic disability but rather as a different way of being. So the NCA teachers and trainers base their lessons on non-judgemental acceptance and respect for individuals. The NCA also organizes fun events like holiday camps and musical concerts to provide all-round exposure. It networks with other organizations concerned with autism in India and abroad. For example, the NCA works closely with the Sarva Shiksha Abhiyan, which is a government agency that provides guidance to autistic children in government schools. It is involved in advocacy and spreading awareness about autism. It assists other countries in South Asia to develop services to help autists and their families as well as get legal recognition of autism.

Raising funds for the activities of the NCA is a contin-ual work. Funds are raised through donations, mainly from corporates as a part of their social responsibility programmes, as well as through fund-raising events and the normal income-based fees charged by the centre for some of its programmes.

Challenges and the Future

Reflecting on her life with an autistic child and the future, Merry says: 'Life has been challenging, but I learnt wonder-ful lessons. For example, I learnt that there is no child who cannot learn and progress, but one has to learn to cele-brate the tiniest steps forward, instead of expecting a big leap. When people see Neeraj now, they marvel at all that he is able to do. From total inability to control himself, Neeraj can now exercise self-control. But there was a time when six men could not hold Neeraj down to give him an injection. Life with Neeraj is still not easy. Every ounce of my resources will be required to ensure that he leads a ful-filling life even when I am no longer there. Has Neeraj changed me as a person? Undoubtedly, and for the better. A big learning was through letting go of expectations. I learnt about sensitivity, patience, and respect in a way that I could not have had learnt otherwise. My son taught me to accept "non-conditionality" in the true sense of the word. I was able to tell my child: "I will do everything in my power to help you learn and grow; but whatever you are, what-ever you do, whatever you become, I love and accept you for just what you are. If I had to live my life again would I want Neeraj to be different? Would I want him to not be autistic?" My answer to both questions is an emphatic "No". There are joys and there are sorrows, there are highs and there are lows, there are challenges and there are triumphs everyday! I lead a very effortful life. But I would not change it for anything. What would happen to Neeraj after I am no longer there? I do not know. I am doing the best I can, taking action to set up services that will look out for our children after us. I do not know whether I will be able to achieve all this in my lifetime or not. But I do know that I will not make myself unhappy worrying about it now.'

For what she has done to help autists and their families, Merry has received national and international recognition. She explains: 'I do this work because I do not want other parents to go through what I went through after Neeraj's diagnosis: the uncertainty, the misinformation and the lack of services. It has been my privilege to help a large number of families.' But Merry feels that her mission is far from accomplished. In spite of the work done in the past 20 years, autism is still not appropriately treated by the medical community. Doctors often display lack of awareness and understanding. They misdiagnose or underdiagnose the condition, sometimes telling parents that their children will outgrow it, when in fact early intervention is crucial, or they give an overly pessimistic view of the child's future. Also, autism is still not fully comprehended by the general public, which often dismisses it as a disorder resulting from 'Western' social values affecting mainly the rich and caused by bad parenting. Such ideas hurt the interests of persons with autism.

So a lot still needs to be done for addressing autism-related issues in India and in neighbouring countries. Merry's mission for the future is based on research, which indicates that people with autism need specialized teaching in communication and social understanding rather than medication and that the most effective teachers can be the parents of autistic children. The challenge is to create ways by which parents can be inducted into the rehabilitation process as teachers, trainers, assessors, etc., to support autistic children, their own and others'.

What is required is teams of dedicated and trained parent specialists who would establish and manage autism support units in dispersed parts of the country. These parent-managed support units would receive support from the NCA, which would serve as a source of tried and tested techniques and methods for dealing with autism. The creation of such a large and diversified transnational organization is a major challenge that would greatly benefit autists and their caretakers as well as society at large. It would also provide Merry with worthwhile work, which would lead to fulfilling her vision of creating a society that recognizes the interdependence of people of every ability as valuable while providing equal opportunities for all.

3

Lakshmi Krishnan

NGO for Empowerment of Women

In many parts of India, even today, if an adolescent girl begets a child out of wedlock, her own kin forsake her and she is condemned to a life of stigma and shame, often with no choice but to abandon the child, which further accentuates her misery. For Lakshmi Krishnan, a sensitive social worker, it was impossible to continue leading a normal work-life since she was aware of the prevalence of such a barbaric behaviour in our society, particularly after she was approached for help by a young girl who had an illegitimate child and had been abandoned by everyone: the girl had no clue about how to take care of her new-born child or how to cope with her own life, which had become a nightmare. Lakshmi was devastated when this experience was shared with her, and she knew then that she had to do something for such girls and their children. It became her mission in life to establish a social welfare organization to help adolescent unwed mothers and their children. After surmounting considerable challenges, her mission was achieved: The Society for the Protection of Women and Children (SPOWAC) was created in 1998. Lakshmi Krishnan is Founder President of the society; other Board members are eminent and respected people from the field of social work.

Lakshmi Krishnan had spent most of her working life caring for destitute children. She graduated in home science with child psychology as her main subject, because she had always been fascinated by children. She obtained her master's degree in social work from the Delhi School of Social Work in 1979 and started her work career there by helping at the school's Child Guidance Clinic while she was still studying. After attaining her master's degree, Lakshmi joined the Khrist Raja Family Helper Project of the Convent of Jesus and Mary School where her responsibilities included helping students from the less privileged sections of society to become integrated in school life by interacting with the parents as well as by arranging help with matters such as books and uniforms. She worked at the convent for four years. While she was there, she learnt about a vacancy at the SOS Children's Villages of India. This respected and high-profile NGO in the area of child welfare was looking for a person to manage its adoption centre. The job description attracted Lakshmi immensely. She knew that she could do the job well, and it was the kind of work she had always wanted. The job required traits in which she was strong, like understanding of and love for children. SOS had a strict recruitment procedure, which included interviews by their directors who were well-known people in the world of social work, such as Tara Ali Baig and J.N. Kaul. Lakshmi recalls that she was nervous when she went for the interview; however, her earnestness and her obvious understanding of children showed up clearly at the interview, and she was selected.

Lakshmi was appointed head of the SOS Adoption Centre—Udayan in the Gole Market area of New Delhi in 1984 when she was 27 years old; she did not realize then that she would remain with Udayan for the next 20 years! It was a life full of hectic activity as well as stress. At any point of time, there were more than 20 children at the centre, many with problematic backgrounds and serious illnesses.

When Lakshmi joined Udayan, she was confronted with her first sociocultural challenge as a young working woman. She had to face the hostile behaviour of staff who were much older than her and had served the organization for long periods and therefore resented the appointment of a young inexperienced girl (called a *kal ki chhokri*) as the boss. Lakshmi overcame this challenge mainly by working harder and with more dedication than her older subordinates. In fact, she set an example by establishing a high standard of conduct and thus demonstrated that she deserved to be in charge.

Incidentally, Lakshmi had two little children of her own to take care of at her home. She recalls that often she was torn between emergencies at Udayan and at her own home and had to oscillate between the two, sometimes late at night and in her nightclothes! Every day presented some new challenge for Lakshmi. Often, the police would bring to Udayan infants who had been abandoned in front of temples or hospitals or even in dustbins! And then it became Lakshmi's responsibility to build the lives of these hapless children.

For example, there was the case of Nilima, an infant who had been abandoned presumably because her genital configuration indicated transgender symptoms and was brought to Udayan. Lakshmi took the child to the All India Institute of Medical Sciences to find out what could be done to help the child. When she returned to Udayan, she found that a large unruly mob of eunuchs had surrounded the entrance and were demanding that the infant be handed over to them as it belonged to their 'community'. Lakshmi single-handedly confronted the crowd and demanded to know from the eunuchs: 'What life will you give to this girl? With you, she will only learn to beg, but if she stays with me I will ensure that she gets education and is able to make a life for herself. In fact if you have more such infants in your "community," please bring them to me and I will help them to get a better life.' The eunuchs blessed Lakshmi and left her alone. Incidentally, Nilima now lives in Europe with her foster parents and has had all the procedures done to ensure that she will grow into a full-fledged woman.

There was also the case of Ramu who had been abandoned by his parents because of a major physical deformity that prevented him from passing stool in the normal way. The parents had tried a colostomy operation, but this had not worked and must have been quite expensive. Lakshmi took the child for care in Udayan, and Ramu was quite soon adopted by a kind and caring couple who arranged for all the necessary treatment for Ramu so that he soon began leading a normal life.

During the two decades with the adoption centre, Lakshmi was involved in the rehabilitation of many children. Lakshmi often managed to do wonders for these children, and in many cases, the kids under her care got better lives than generally available to average Indian children of even well-to-do families. Many children were adopted by foreign parents and then lived in homes in Europe and America and received quality education, which helped them build successful careers and even raise families.

For many years, even after she had left Udayan, Lakshmi continued to get letters from children who had been with her. Many of these were letters of thanks for her help in finding them happy homes. However, there were also many letters from the children requesting her to help them contact their natural parents; such letters were distressing for Lakshmi because although she could sympathize with the desire of a child to establish contact with their natural parents, she had also to be sensitive to the delicate protocol of the adoption process and the feelings of the natural parents as well as the new parents. One boy who was brought to the adoption centre in very dire circumstances and later adopted by a European couple wrote a long affectionate letter to Lakshmi enquiring about Udayan and also asked: 'How does it feel when children leave? Are you happy or sad?' Lakshmi replied: 'The bonding is strong. I am both happy and sad. I am happy because I know that the child is going to a good home. The sadness is for a short time because there are other children who need my attention and care.' That more or less sums up her attitude to her work.

Lakshmi left Udayan in 2003. During her 20 years there, she had faced a variety of challenges, gained rich experience and developed strong self-confidence. She felt ready to build her own organization, according to her own ideas and values rather than those of SOS. Of course, SOS had given her a free hand in handling Udayan because of her exceptional capabilities, which had been highly appreciated. But being given a free hand is still very different from being the boss. Lakshmi began devoting time and attention to building SPOWAC. It had already been registered as an NGO during her last years with SOS. Its main objective was to provide support to unwed adolescent mothers and their children. This included rehabilitation of the young mothers through training, counseling and other activities to empower them to face life as well as arranging care for the children. It also included creating awareness in society about the demeaning consequences of intolerance as well as promoted modern liberal ideas so that future generations could live in a civilized culture. The objectives of SPOWAC were expanded later to include certain other social issues to obtain the support of some major donors like the Delhi government. However, the main objective of SPOWAC continued to be caring for adolescent unwed mothers and their children.

Although SPOWAC's objectives were highly appreciated, the wherewithal to establish the organization and run its activities was totally beyond the reach of the resources available with Lakshmi. In fact, she had no resources at all, apart from a very strong will power as well as a passionate desire to empower women in distress and support helpless children. Fortunately, the praise and accolades from the government and organizations concerned with human welfare were often backed by donations and other forms of help. For example, as an active member of the Inner Wheel Club, an affiliate of Rotary International, Lakshmi leveraged the network to obtain help for SPOWAC projects. Also, she was able to persuade the Municipal Corporation of Delhi to allot some accommodation to SPOWAC in the Community Centre at Multani Dhanda, a poor and congested area of Paharganj in central Delhi. All this support enabled SPOWAC to create the organization and infrastructure to start delivering welfare programmes.

In 2006, SPOWAC was selected by the Delhi government to be the nodal agency to implement its welfare schemes for helping the vulnerable sections of society in the central districts of Delhi. These schemes are now managed by SPOWAC from the Multani Dhanda office. The amalgamation of the schemes in one office has greatly benefitted the poor in central Delhi. The office includes a facilitation desk, which serves as a single window to provide guidance about various welfare schemes. Apart from providing information, this desk facilitates filling forms, conducts initial scrutiny and forwards applications to the appropriate authorities.

SPOWAC has launched several major welfare programmes from its tiny office in Multani Dhanda, including vocational training and skill development courses to empower the young unwed mothers so that they can become economically independent. These six-month courses include tailoring, embroidery, beauty culture, mehendi decorating, computer literacy, cooking and various arts and crafts. Girls who had no schooling or had dropped out from school are encouraged to attend non-formal education classes that provide functional literacy. To bring social awareness into the lives of these girls, SPOWAC arranges get-togethers, excursions and picnics. Care for their children is carried out through a programme of rehabilitation, which includes adoption and arranging foster homes as well as repatriation to parents. SPOWAC also organizes remedial teaching classes at various places to enable children to enhance their interest in studies as well as to do homework. It conducts weekly free health clinics with OPD facilities. Monthly nutrition camps create awareness about low-cost diets and cooking methods that retain the nutritional value of food. Legal awareness camps educate poor people about their rights and provide free counselling. Comprehensive health insurance is provided to poor families at a nominal premium. Self-help groups are encouraged to promote self-sufficiency and to encourage women to collectively solve their problems; some of these groups provide micro credit; some others produce items like non-plastic bags to promote a healthy environment, with SPOWAC helping with the marketing.

SPOWAC is also commissioned from time to time to undertake research assignments and studies in its area of work. For example, it conducted a baseline survey to create a database of the vulnerable sections of society in designated areas of Delhi. This project involved visiting individual households and recording information about economic and social parameters. Such assignments contribute to promoting awareness about issues that are of concern to SPOWAC as well as generate funds for its activities. SPOWAC also raises funds through its popular cultural programmes, which feature young upcoming artistes, many of whom are now becoming national celebrities.

Lakshmi comes from a family of civil service officials. She was born in Mumbai in 1957. When she was seven years old, she moved to Delhi following her father's transfer. She got married in Delhi to a businessman who owned a clearing and forwarding firm. Her husband did not get involved in Lakshmi's social welfare work, although he provided moral support. He did, however, once make a very significant contribution to Lakshmi's project, though unwittingly. This was with respect to the shocking case of a three-year-old girl who had been tied up in a gunny bag after being brutally mutilated and left in a railway train compartment with the obvious intention of letting her die. The police found her and brought her to Lakshmi. The girl remained in a state of shock for many days and would not respond to any help—she just stared continuously and expressionlessly at the ceiling and showed no interest in anything. When Lakshmi's husband happened to drop by, he saw this girl in a sad state and instinctively gave her a big affectionate smile. That smile from a benevolent-looking man did wonders for her. She began to take an interest in her surroundings and responding to care. Apparently, she had not received such a smile in her painful past! Since the girl had no name, Lakshmi gave her a name—Savitri. Under Lakshmi's loving care, Savitri grew into a charming intelligent girl. Later, she was adopted by a Swedish couple and then lived and studied in Stockholm. Many years later, Savitri did get a chance to meet up with Lakshmi when Lakshmi happened to be in Sweden in connection with some other adoptions. Lakshmi says that she was delighted to see that Savitri had grown into a graceful young lady and was doing very well in her studies.

During the course of her long career in social work, Lakshmi has written several papers and has been a resource person at seminars concerning child welfare. She has also featured in the print media and on television programmes. She has produced a documentary film titled *Blissful Parenting*, which deals with the socio-psychological issues regarding child adoption. Lakshmi is now respected as a thinker, activist and advocate on family and child welfare issues. Incidentally, a major contribution to Lakshmi's personal growth and development came from travelling abroad. Many foreign adoption centres insist on an adopted child being escorted to their country to facilitate integration. Lakshmi had often been the obvious choice to be the escort, and she used these opportunities to learn about what was happening in her area of work in other countries as well as to meet some of the children who had been looked after by her and happened to be living in the area. Such travel helped Lakshmi to be well informed about the latest and best practices related to the welfare of disadvantaged children.

Regarding the sociocultural challenges that women encounter in her kind of work, Lakshmi says: 'Dealing with petty bureaucrats such as inspectors from regulatory agencies and enforcement authorities exposes women to crude behaviour; she speaks of many instances of "passes" being made at women accompanied by improper advances. This is a widespread practice, though not often spoken about. The way to deal with this evil, she believes, is to ensure that it is widely known that the woman is protected by the an organization and the state and any misbehavior will certainly be punished.'

At SPOWAC, Lakshmi has created an organization of dedicated staff who share her missionary zeal and compassion. Her son Sriram is a graduate and is currently working at the Multani Dhanda office. He is involved and dedicated, but Lakshmi feels that there are not enough opportunities and resources to gainfully employ a talented young man who should be getting ready to embark on an active career. Sriram, however, appears quite happy doing social welfare work and supplementing his income through short-term assignments with some corporates. Incidentally, SPOWAC also associates with other social welfare organizations that have similar aims. Management students from Business Schools come to SPOWAC for internships. Student social workers and volunteers form a part of the SPOWAC organization.

The Future

Now that SPOWAC has the infrastructure, the organization and the experience of conducting various types of programmes particularly for the empowerment of women and for looking after destitute children, Lakshmi has been considering the future development of SPOWAC. She wishes that gradually SPOWAC's ideology and mission should prevail in many parts of India.

Lakshmi believes that in her kind of activity, it is more effective to grow by replicating a successful project rather than expanding it. To facilitate this process, the board of SPOWAC has recently been expanded to include like-minded people from other Indian states to facilitate the replication of SPOWAC, particularly by entering rural India, which she considers to be the nerve centre of the country. This process has been started by establishing a welfare centre in a small village in the Palwal district of Haryana. This centre focuses on education, health and sanitation. There is another SPOWAC project centre in a poor and congested resettlement colony near Dwarka in Southwest Delhi, and similar welfare activities will be conducted there from premises that have been made available by the local municipality in a Basti Vikas Kendra. Centres in other places will require benefactors like state governments, philanthropic organizations or corporates to nurture the local centre financially. Finding such sponsors is one of Lakshmi's major tasks. In fact, finding sponsors for SPOWAC's activities has always been a major and continual challenge for Lakshmi, which takes up a lot of her time. Fortunately, she is gifted with personal charm, and when this is combined with her obvious integrity and commitment to her cause, it makes her a very persuasive and effective fund-raiser.

When asked about why she decided to devote her life to social work, Lakshmi laughs: 'The returns on investment of time are tremendous in terms of spiritual satisfaction, and when this satisfaction is combined with the physical exhaustion of working very hard every day, it results in good sleep every night, and that's a big reward!'

She is also convinced that her career has developed through the working out of destiny: she never deliberately planned her career moves; rather she let her career unfold and philosophically accepted the position in which she was placed by making the most of it.

4

Sudha Sastri

HR Consultancy

MBA students often say that they would like to start their own business after gathering some work experience; however, very few actually manage to do this. They are tempted to remain employed because of the security of regular pay cheques and growing family responsibilities.

Sudha is an example of an MBA who first gained a few years' experience in the corporate world and then went on to start her own business—although that was not quite the way she had planned it! In fact, her career underwent many twists and turns as well as turnarounds before she finally settled into a business.

Sudha is the founder and president of Inputs, a leading human relations (HR) solutions provider specialized in helping small- and medium-sized enterprises (SMEs) to use the transformative power of HR to overcome challenges in areas such as recruiting, retaining and nurturing talent as well as implementing change for growth.

However, initially, when Sudha started work in the early 1990s, she was in the business of assisting large multinational companies in the IT and telecom sectors that wanted to establish a presence in India to take advantage of the liberalization of the Indian economy. Her clients then included giant international companies who were leaders in their fields such as Oracle, Microsoft, Sun Microsystems, Intel and GE Money.

When new growth opportunities in the Indian economy led to a substantial development in the SME sector, Sudha shifted her focus from foreign MNCs to Indian SMEs. Many SMEs were finding it difficult to promote themselves into the big league mainly because of certain managerial inadequacies; Sudha's mission was to identify these inadequacies and help these SMEs overcome them. She says: 'Many entrepreneur-led start-ups, especially in sectors like IT, IT-enabled services, telecom, education and healthcare, grew rapidly, but as annual sales moved up to about ₹10 million they began to struggle with people challenges. I saw vast opportunities in helping these companies to adopt appropriate practices so that they could realize their potential.'

The Formative Years

Sudha's childhood and schooling were at Jamshedpur where her father headed Industrial Engineering at the Tata Iron & Steel Company (TISCO). He was a principled man, and his style of dealing with contentious issues such as fixing standards for determining incentives, which always excite both management and workers, earned him the respect of both the TISCO management and the Tata Workers' Union. Sudha says that many of the values that she brings to her work developed through watching him. For example, she learnt from him about standing up for what one believes to be right, even in the face of strong contrarian opinions. Sudha's mother was a physics teacher and vice principal of a school in Jamshedpur. Of her two brothers, one studied at IIT Chennai and IIM Kolkata, attained a PhD from Wharton and then went on to become a tenured professor at the Harvard Business School. The other brother studied at IIM Ahmedabad, worked for some top banks and then became a partner in an invest-ment bank in Mumbai. This may not be the usual family background that one associates with a typical struggling woman entrepreneur, but it partly explains why Sudha's venture is somewhat unusual.

Sudha studied management at IIM Kolkata from 1983 to 1985. In those days, students of the two-year MBA course chose their specialization in the second year. Sudha ini-tially chose electives in finance because she fancied a career in that area. In those days, human relations devel-opment was not a very popular option with MBA students, most of whom preferred finance or marketing as they felt these led to better placement possibilities. However at IIM Kolkata, Sudha learnt that people-oriented subjects like HR were now being handled very professionally and could lead to rewarding careers. She soon became aware that she had an affinity for HR and would like to work in that area. Through the campus placement process, she secured a position in HR with Eicher India Ltd in New Delhi, and the job delighted her: She found Eicher to be a company with enlightened HR practices, which convinced her that her decision to opt for HR was right for her. She recalls working with and learning from leading professionals like Anil Sachdev, who was then setting HR standards at Eicher.

In 1986, Sudha married Srikant Sastri, a class fellow from IIM Kolkata, who was then working with Ponds as a marketing manager. Srikant was then based in Chennai, and Sudha resigned from Eicher to make their new home. In Chennai, Sudha joined a human resources and organizational development consultancy firm specializing in change management. Like many such firms in those days, this firm made recommendations to corporates regarding strategies, structures and systems for coping with change but did not get involved in the implementation of its recommendations. Sudha was not happy working there because she preferred being involved in issues from start to finish—in all aspects of a change programme through ideating, strategizing, securing buy-ins from concerned parties and then helping with implementing the change, even if this involved working inside the organization for the duration of the change process.

Fortunately for Sudha, after six months in Chennai, Srikant was transferred to New Delhi and the couple moved again. Sudha joined Pertech Computers in New Delhi. This was a start-up with respect to many of its new activities. Pertech's HR organization was divided into HR Management and HR Development. The former included mainly personnel administration, whereas the latter dealt with strategies and policies. Sudha headed the latter and was given a lot of freedom to implement her ideas. She enjoyed the work immensely. In fact, it was in the innovative, freethinking atmosphere of this start-up that Sudha got attracted to the idea of establishing her own start-up as an entrepreneur.

In 1990, Sudha had her first baby; it was a complicated premature delivery, and the baby was often unwell. Nursing the baby became the most important activity in her life involving a lot of her time. She was then still employed with Pertech. The management there was sympathetic and gave her a year off provided she would continue to drive their training programmes from home. This experience, to a great extent, explains Sudha's sensitivity to the situation of working mothers, which is reflected in some of her business decisions later.

Launching Her Business

In the 1990s when India was liberalizing and opening up its economy, many US-based IT companies were looking for connections with India. Sudha's name was often recommended as a person who could help because of her experience in the HR sector and her knowledge of the IT sector. She began receiving calls from US-based IT companies for HR-oriented assignments. One day, a friend called to ask whether she could help AT&T hire key managers in India. Such enquiries encouraged Sudha to explore the possibility of starting her own consultancy business. In 1992, she finally quit Pertech and started her own consultancy firm Inputs, which commenced business from their home in Munirka Vihar; the staff then comprised just Sudha.

In 1995, Srikant left his job to start his own business. Since his student days at IIM Kolkata, it had been his ambition to be an entrepreneur, and so he decided to implement his plan of quitting employment after acquiring some experience in the corporate world. About those times Sudha says: 'My husband and I had sold all our assets and withdrawn our provident funds to kick start his business. We were living off what I was earning because his business was slow in taking off. In fact we had no money to invest in my business.' Sudha then often wondered then whether it was more difficult to be an entrepreneur or to be an entrepreneur's wife! She concluded that being an entrepreneur's wife was more difficult because she got little information and no control on the cash flows affecting the financing of day-to-day home expenses.

In 1996, Microsoft, from its US office, approached Sudha for help in outsourcing some recruitment processes. This was a major breakthrough as well as a big opportunity for Sudha and a turning point for Inputs. However, it then became necessary for Sudha to have a well-appointed office. Inputs moved to a new office in Nehru Place—the posh commercial centre in South Delhi; and Inputs grew from being just a self-employed individual to being a company with an office.

Those were very difficult times for Sudha. There were heavy developmental expenses, little income and a lot of hard work. Around that time, Sudha was expecting her second baby and was put on bed rest frequently. In 1997, Sudha gave birth to her second baby. She said: 'Having had my first child before schedule, I should have been prepared for the next one arriving early. However, when the baby arrived a month early, I was unprepared. The day I went into labour many interviews had been scheduled. So between contractions, I was on the phone with my clients! It was again a difficult pregnancy. I was tempted to give up my business. But my husband's business was yet to take off and we needed the income. So, I ploughed on.'

Overcoming Challenges

Women entrepreneurs often face a variety of challenges in starting and running their businesses, and Sudha had her share of problems, which she dealt with using her distinctive approach, style and attitude:

BUILDING THE ORGANIZATION

Most women entrepreneurs face the challenge of finding the right people for their start-ups. This difficulty arises from the perception that start-ups take time to pay attractive salaries, and there is also the lurking fear that the business may fold up if the woman owner quits to start a family.

For Inputs, Sudha created a distinctive organizational structure. It was based on her belief that in India, there is considerable untapped management talent in women who are highly qualified, knowledgeable and experienced and were star executives in the corporate sector till they gave up employment after marriage and children. Many of these women have excellent management education, professional training and rich experience. Sudha decided to build her organization around such women by providing them with an appropriate working environment. She allowed these 'working moms' to have flexible working hours, to work from home and to choose the consultancy assignments with which they would feel comfortable considering their home commitments.

This unique organizational structure and work regime enabled Sudha to tap into a big reservoir of talent. Her team was highly motivated and devoted, which was one of the main reasons for the success of Inputs. Flexibility in working hours was a key driver, but it also made planning a nightmare and often interesting assignments had to be turned down. Incidentally, Sudha implemented this organizational strategy long before the Tatas thought up the concept of the Second Life Plan, which also aimed at hiring women who had left executive positions in the corporate sector to care for families.

Managing the Home and Family

To a great extent, being able to manage one's time while establishing and running a business venture depends upon the attitude of the family. Regarding the attitude of her own family, Sudha says: 'Very supportive! Especially my mother, and my mother-in-law, who often did nanny duty. However, like most Indian women, even if they are the breadwinners, the primary responsibility for home and kids was always mine and so I had to deal with the dual responsibility of running a home and a business. The business had to pay the price more often than not. As the kids were growing they were happy to see me involved in my work. My husband Srikant was always strongly supportive of my business, partly because of his own entrepreneurial interests.'

Both Sudha and her husband fortunately shared common values and ideas about what brings happiness. Making a lot of money quickly did not feature in either's goals.

Raising Finance and Overcoming Bureaucratic Hurdles

Often, banks in India view women entrepreneurs as risky clients, but Sudha managed her business in such a way that she did not depend on external finances, and so she was spared the embarrassment of pleading her case to sceptical bank managers. With respect to bureaucratic hurdles, Sudha says: 'Getting the approvals, permissions, licences, registrations to start a business can often be a harrowing experience. For dealing with the MCD, the police, tax authorities most business people resort to paying bribes just to avoid harassment.' However, here again, Sudha was relatively unaffected, because her work did not involve many dealings with governmental agencies, and in any case, she had decided that Inputs' approach would be based on principled conduct.

Positioning the Business

How would Inputs deal with the matter of adding value to the client's business? Sudha feels that market compulsions are forcing companies to change, but there is often a resistance to change because of cultural issues. A change intervention could be sound, but it would not work if it clashed with a company's culture. Sudha believes that many corporate leaders do not pay sufficient attention to the way their company's core culture is perceived, and misunderstandings result through wrong strategic decisions. She says: 'You ask employees to use five adjectives to describe their company's core culture and you will be amazed at the lack of agreement that exists. Many companies wish to become employers of choice for talented individuals. For this to happen employees' aspirations and value systems should be in sync with those of the company. Employees are happiest when they are able to identify fully with the company's culture.'

Therefore, much of Inputs' value addition is concerned with working on the company's core culture and its perception.

The structure of Inputs is simple. It is a proprietary concern. There are very few full-time paid employees on the rolls of Inputs. The professional consultancy work is carried out by the 'working moms'. Sudha is the chief executive, and by and large, initial business development is carried out by her. For each new client, one of the of the network consultants is appointed as the account manager and is responsible for serving and mining the account. She is responsible for all aspects of the assignment including delivery and client satisfaction and receives 50 per cent of the invoice value as her share.

Personal Matters

What is striking about Sudha is her people orientation. Apart from being an engaging and persuasive conversationalist, she is an avid listener. In fact, she is practically an agony aunt and a confidante to everyone—from candidates to clients, as well as her sons and their friends and even their friends' mothers!

What makes Sudha different from other 'IIM-types'? In many important ways, she is similar, not different. For instance, she is a strong believer in achievement and playing to win. She is also a strong believer in good old values like integrity, principled conduct, punctuality and meeting commitments.

Sudha's entrepreneurial experience of running an HR Consultancy has led to her acceptance of certain theses that she constantly evangelizes: first, women need not choose between business and family—they can do both; second, women often have to respond to circumstances and create opportunities out of them, unlike men who manage situations in a more planned and structured environment; and third, women entrepreneurs do not have to fall in line with traditional venture capitalist frameworks.

Sudha's advice to aspiring entrepreneurs is that they should work for five or more years in an established setup related to their proposed line of business before starting off on their own. Her experience, and her knowledge of others, has left her convinced that there is no substitute for real-world experience, especially for first-generation entrepreneurs.

The Future

Sudha believes that the success of Inputs should be measured by the quality of its services, its values and its integrity rather than by its top and bottom lines. Realizing that it is easier to ensure quality in a smaller organization, she has decided not to aim for large size. 'Better and better' she says, 'rather than, bigger and bigger'.

Sudha would like to enlarge her network of consultants to other cities, but she does not intend to go around looking for business in foreign countries. She feels that India will soon become a focal point in the world for acquiring and developing talent and that companies like Inputs will have a bright future and enough to do right here in India without having to set up an organization to search for business in foreign countries.

Now that she has her own successful business, Sudha cannot think of doing anything different, and she would find it impossible to ever work as an employee again. .She says: 'I am having a blast; I cannot imagine doing it any other way.' The flexibility in her approach to business allows Sudha to do many things. Apart from being a hands-on mother, she has been mentoring a boxer who was then training for the Olympics. The person was none other than the renowned Mary Com. She says that it was one of the most satisfying experiences of her life. She has two sons. The older one studied at Brown University in the US and is now working in India with Bain & Company, consultants—a favourite of the GenNext community. The younger one is studying at Shri Ram School in New Delhi. 'I will help and encourage them to be free spirits who have the courage to follow their hearts and be great human beings.'

Looking back at her working life over the past 20 years, Sudha marvels at the journey. She became an entrepreneur through a series of fortuitous circumstances. She calls herself 'an entrepreneur by default'. When she started Inputs, there was no clear vision and certainly no definitive business plan. Growth was random. She recalls: 'When the first phone call came about work for US companies I had no intention of starting a business. Seemingly preordained events kept happening and I now seriously believe that it is wiser to open oneself to be moved and to flow with the tide, rather than force issues.'

5

Ritu Prasad

Hospitality

Ritu is the founder and chief executive of 'Spirit': a wining and dining restaurant in a posh part of New Delhi. The restaurant covers 25,000 square feet of prime commercial space in the inner circle of Connaught Place, with a seating capacity for 75 guests. It has a staff of 50

members and a management team comprising a general manager, an executive chef and functional managers. The restaurant specializes in gourmet cuisine from countries bordering the Mediterranean and has a regular upmarket clientele mainly comprising Indian and foreign business executives.

Ritu's achievement is admirable when one considers the challenges that she had to overcome in her entrepreneurial journey: First, she came from a traditional Jain family of total teetotallers and strict vegetarians, so there were many raised eyebrows about her involvement with liquor and wines as well as with steaks and joints, which happened to be the preferred fare of Spirit's executive and business clientele. Second, she had no training or experience in food and beverages management and neither was she exceptionally fond of cooking, although she enjoyed good food and a nice ambience. Third, just when the restaurant had taken off and was beginning to do well, she suffered a spinal injury that paralyzed the lower half of her body, making her seriously disabled. She then had to run her business from a wheelchair.

Ritu managed to overcome the challenges in her entrepreneurial career mainly because of certain strong personality traits. Her dominant personality traits are a zest for adventure, creativity and variety. She has a cheerful disposition and a witty sense of humour that help her and her family deal with issues that arise from her physical disability. Because of her disposition, she finds it difficult to engage in routine, dull work in a bureaucratic, hierarchical organization. Like many well-known entrepreneurs, she trusts her gut feelings; she also likes quick decisions. (Incidentally she took 15 minutes to consent to marrying Rohit Prasad after their first meeting in the 'arranged marriage' process, although her family had advised her to take more time and have more meetings.) She is endowed with an entrepreneurial spirit that propels her to constantly seek out business opportunities. Even while holidaying, her mind is occupied with questions like 'what are the opportunities here?'

The Formative Years

Ritu's schooling was at the Convent of Jesus and Mary in New Delhi. As a young girl, she was attracted to the sciences and wanted to study medicine and become a doctor. Her father was supportive of this plan provided she got admission to a medical college in Delhi. This did not come about because these colleges had few seats, many of which were reserved. Ritu then sought admission into the Economics (Honours) course at the Lady Sri Ram College for Women (LSR), University of Delhi, mainly because this was a much coveted course and because friends and relatives advised her that it was appropriate for a person of her background. She gained admission there, but she had no interest in economics and found the course a big bore and of little relevance to what she was looking for in life.

After graduating from LSR in 1990, Ritu did a Post Graduate Diploma in Management from the Sydenham Institute of Management Studies (SIMS) in Mumbai. Shifting to Mumbai involved taking up paying guest accommodation near her college, off Marine Drive. She enjoyed her stay in Mumbai, and her two years at the B-School proved to be a great learning experience for her. Amongst other things, they revealed to her what she was good at—marketing and advertising. Her entrepreneurial capabilities also unfolded: even while she was still a student, she set herself up as a consultant and did some paid research studies in the area of comparative brand awareness for advertising agencies such as Lintas and Ogilvy & Mather (O&M) as well as for FMCG companies. Through these consultancy assignments, which were her first entrepreneurial business venture, she earned pocket money, which she spent mainly on good food in good restaurants and thus gained insights that would prove useful in her business ventures later.

After Ritu completed the course at SIMS in 1992, her father summoned her to Delhi to work with him in his business, which concerned engineering projects in steel plants. So, unlike many of her colleagues, she did not take advantage of the campus placement process and she left the college without an appointment letter from a major corporate. She did not feel comfortable in her father's business because it had nothing to do with what she liked and the work was not in sync with her personality. In fact, she viewed the move from SIMS to her father's business as a retrograde step. (Later in life, she would discover that being summoned to Delhi to join her father's business was probably one of the best things ever to happen to her—more about that later.)

With respect to what was taught at the B-School, Ritu says she found the courses concerned with how to build, motivate and lead a team—as well as how to persuade and negotiate—most useful. She says: 'These people-skills, taught in the organization development and human resources courses, are always helpful in start-ups particularly in the hospitality business.' In her restaurant, one can see the importance attached to customer service; the waiters go out of their way to explain the intricacies of each dish on the menu, which is a sign that there has been emphasis on coaching by a person who understands concepts such as 'delighting customers'.

Regarding other subjects taught at B-Schools, Ritu felt that many of the more intricate topics in finance were of little practical value for start-ups. However, some of the less intricate topics like cash-flow management were very helpful. She also learnt useful concepts in operations management, particularly those dealing with systems and controls, which later helped her in managing her business. She says: 'If I had not done my MBA, and if I had started my business immediately after my degree—I would have found the going extremely difficult.'

After a year in her father's business, she decided to quit and applied to O&M for a job in Delhi. She was selected immediately and enjoyed the job immensely. Her work involved the advertising accounts of Reckitt & Coleman, Seagrams and *Hindustan Times*. She did not mind the long hours, often more than 10 hours a day, because she found the work great fun—it involved dealing with the launch of new products and with new business ideas, so there was much variety and excitement as well as scope for creativity, which had always been very important to her.

When Ritu was to get married in 1995, it was considered imperative in her family circles that she discontinue her hectic work routine. In fact, neither her parents nor her in-laws thought that it would be proper for her to work anymore. So she quit her job at O&M. Her husband, Rohit Prasad, was a successful chartered accountant who had started a financial services company in partnership with his brother a few years earlier. Ritu and Rohit managed to persuade the families to agree that after being the typical Jain bahu for a reasonable period of time, Ritu would work in her husband's financial services company. This, however, did not materialize because of various intrafamily issues, so in fact Ritu had no work after marriage.

Realizing Ritu's predicament and her need to be active, her husband supported her efforts to start some work. She took up an assignment with 'I Discovery'—a small private company started by a few XLRI (Xavier School of Management) alumni for running summer camps for school children. Ritu enjoyed the opportunity to be involved with this unusual start-up because it suited her temperament and her inclinations, but she had to quit after a year for health reasons.

Rohit well understood that exciting and creative activity was necessary for Ritu; he also knew she had a flair for finding business opportunities and taking advantage of them. He had noted how as a student at B-School in Mumbai, she had seen that advertising agencies and companies marketing FMCG products would gladly pay for studies related to perceptions of the brand personalities of competing products and how she had then offered consultancy services as a successful business venture.

Starting Business

In those days Delhi, unlike Mumbai, had very few specialty stand-alone restaurants. The best restaurants were found in expensive five-star hotels. Ritu saw a business opportunity to tap the market provided by people in Delhi who wanted to have high-quality gourmet cuisine without having to pay exorbitant five-star hotel prices. Her gut feeling informed her that a restaurant offering such fare would do well. She also felt that she would enjoy establishing and running such a restaurant, and she felt confident that she could make a success of it. So she decided to go for it.

No formal market research was conducted and no project report was prepared. It was mainly a gut feeling. However, Ritu did conduct some informal research herself. The first issue to be settled was the kind of food the restaurant would offer. She noted that Delhi already had many restaurants serving Indian cuisine as well as some restaurants, mainly in hotels, offering Chinese and Continental cuisine. She also noticed that cuisine from the Middle East was missing even though north Indians had a natural affinity for that kind of food, particularly for Lebanese dishes. Her personal research in Delhi suggested that her restaurant should focus on cuisine from the Middle East, Lebanon and Morocco as well as from countries bordering the northern Mediterranean.

Ritu then looked at restaurants in other countries. She made two trips to Dubai to check out some restaurants there. Rohit accompanied her to provide advice on the non-vegetarian angle. (As a good Jain, Ritu is a strict vegetarian, although not a strict teetotaller!) In Dubai, Ritu also checked out sources of specialist spices as well as collected ideas relating to décor and ambience: for example, she noted the importance of *sheesha*, which is smoking the hookah, after an Arab meal. On her return from Dubai, she brought back with her a dozen hookahs and managed to convince the Indian Customs that these were brought in not for commercial purposes but for personal use because her extended family was hopelessly addicted to smoking the hookah after meals!

Premises for the restaurant, appropriately to be named 'Spirit', were identified and bought with financial help from her husband, and Spirit was launched in August 2001. However, it soon became clear to Ritu that her lack of experience in food and beverages management would be a major handicap. She appointed the celebrated chef Zachariah from the Taj group of hotels to work with her as a consultant and to deal with matters relating to cuisine and kitchen management. She also appointed a top interior decorator to advise her about décor and ambience. She hired a highly qualified, experienced (and expensive) general manager to look after the operations of the restaurant. This support staff was a great help and also enabled her to learn the 'tricks of the trade'. She is now fully savvy with restaurant and bar operating controls; there is no way that her staff can take her for a ride.

Entrepreneurs establishing small businesses in India face a number of problems, particularly if they are women. The management of the Inspector Raj is a demanding challenge and a major headache for small businesses. Ritu had her share of corrupt petty government officers looking for bribes and freebies. In fact, these officials acted as if it was their right to enjoy expensive food and drinks and not pay for them. Small business owners will tell you that managing corrupt petty bureaucrats and inspectors is a major problem, which requires special skills that are not taught at business schools. Ritu had to learn these skills 'on the job' although the management education did made her confident enough not be bullied or intimidated.

In 2005, Ritu began exploring another business venture. This project involved establishing a mountain resort in Ramgarh in Uttarakhand where Delhi residents could visit for a few days to chill out and relax. The resort would have a distinctive theme based on closeness to nature. It would be located in beautiful surroundings, organically grown delicious food would be served and the guests would be encouraged to pass time close to nature through walks and treks. The homely cottages would have fireplaces with natural fuel-like pine cones. She planned the project in great detail and an idyllic location near Ramgarh was found for the resort and bought.

However, one fateful day while driving to Ramgarh, she met with a terrible car accident that permanently damaged her spine and paralyzed the lower half of her body. Ritu was badly shaken by the accident and felt that she could not go back to her work—her will and her determination had been very adversely affected. But Rohit encouraged her to get back to work. He would take her to Spirit every day and stay at the restaurant providing support. He more or less nursed her back to work. She gradually began to run Spirit again but now from a wheelchair. She personally oversaw all aspects of the restaurant including the menu, the décor and the finances as well as materials management and promotion, she particularly ensured that Spirit stayed ahead of the competition by being innovative, imaginative and in sync with current tastes.

Presently, the restaurant is doing very well and yields good earnings. Of course, there are downturns in times of recessions when the corporate customers, who are a significant part of the clientele, reduce their visits to restaurants. However, the Ramgarh resort project was put on hold.

Personal Matters

Ritu lives in a joint family establishment with her husband, their two school-going children (a boy and a girl) and her parents-in-law. Her mother lives close by. The family is totally supportive of Ritu's business venture since they accept that creative work is a part of her personality. Ritu is very concerned that the children should not feel neglected in any way because of her involvement in business. So she ensures that she sees the kids off to school in the mornings before she leaves for her own work and that she is back at home when the kids return from school. Her husband has been very supportive throughout. He understands and admires her guts and penchant for taking risks—because he himself is an entrepreneur. Although he is supportive of her business endeavours, he is not keenly interested in the details. In fact, when Spirit was being prepared for launch, he did not visit the restaurant till the day of the opening. With respect to the Ramgarh project, Ritu says: 'I doubt whether he is the kind of person who would enjoy spending time at the resort. He likes his busy work life in Delhi and needs to be with his laptop and smartphone. He would be bored in Ramgarh.' But he was a great help throughout by advising Ritu about the commercial issues involved in negotiations with contractors and suppliers as well as in dealing with the regulatory authorities. And, of course, after the accident, he supported her return to work, at a time when she was almost giving up.

Regarding the future, Ritu feels a change is due because between the time that she started Spirit in 2001 and now, there have been major changes in the hospitality business in Delhi. Customers are choosier and there is greater competition. She started Spirit without prior formal market research. This would be unthinkable today. If one has the wrong menu or location or décor, one could be out of business very soon. Indeed, this has happened to many restaurants in Delhi.

There have also been major changes in Ritu's own situation and perceptions. She now feels that Connaught Place, which was once considered upmarket is going downhill fast. Moreover, her lack of mobility makes it difficult to do justice to running a restaurant on the first floor. So Ritu's future plans include possibilities of relocating her restaurant to somewhere in south Delhi where managing from a wheelchair would be less of a problem. The experience of running Spirit has provided her with new ideas that would contribute to the establishment of a different kind of restaurant. For example, her study of restaurant-going people in Delhi informs her that there exists a large unfulfilled demand for 'pubs' where people can get good-quality drinks, including sophisticated liquors and cocktails as well as gourmet snacks in an atmosphere conducive to chatting and bonhomie. She feels that the time is now ripe for such a place. Perhaps it could include a beer brewing facility within the restaurant—a concept that is proving popular in other parts of the world. In fact, she is already checking out this possibility with the regulatory authorities in Delhi.

She would also like to revive the project of the resort in Ramgarh. This would involve commencing development on the five-acre plot that was bought in 2005. She says that she would start on this 'as soon as she has sorted out her ideas about future plans—and got into the mood'.

Looking back at the critical turning points in her career, Ritu considers that a significant decision in her life was to leave Mumbai immediately after SIMS and return to Delhi to join her father's business, although at that time it appeared to be a very retrograde move. In Mumbai, in the 1990s, corporates went out of their way to encourage young marketing and advertising professionals more than in any other city in India. Ritu now realizes that had she stayed back in Mumbai instead of returning to Delhi to join her father's business, she would probably have got a well-paid job with a major corporate, enjoyed her work immensely, become very comfortable with the big salary and perks and then never left employment to start her own business. She has seen this happen to many would-be entrepreneurs. So what she once regarded as a misfortune she now considers a boon.

Concerning advice to young entrepreneurs, Ritu says: 'I think too many young entrepreneurs these days are spending disproportionate time on promoting their business instead of improving their business in terms of quality and value for money.' Ritu sees the importance of healthy top and bottom lines but for her, as founder and owner of Spirit, it is also important to receive positive reports about the quality of the food, the service, the décor and the ambience.

6

Ayesha Grewal

Organic Farming

Ayesha Grewal, a passionate advocate of sustainable development, is the founder of The Altitude Store (TAS), a socially motivated company that helps small farmers in remote hill areas grow and sell sophisticated organic food.

Ayesha's earlier work with village people in India had been concerned with rural development and the creation of livelihoods that were economically and ecologically beneficial. She had noticed then that many small farmers in hilly areas such as Uttarakhand had, for centuries, followed traditional organic farming methods but earned little because they did not have access to markets where they would be paid reasonable prices for their superior merchandize. At the same time, people in urban markets such as Delhi were clamouring for organic food, which they found difficult to obtain even though they were willing to pay appropriate prices. TAS was conceived as the enabling bridge that would serve both the producers and the consumers of organic food.

Background

Ayesha's father had a distinguished career as a finance executive in the corporate world, reaching a high position in Citibank. Rising further in the bank would have involved moving out of India. He preferred to skip the promotion and stay on in India because both husband and wife were keen that their two daughters grow up in Indian surroundings and culture. Later, Mr Grewal was picked up by the Tatas for their hotel company. In 1983, he bought a farm, where he later practised organic farming. Ayesha spent much time at this farm and enjoyed experimenting with new ways of growing things. So the organic way was a part of Ayesha's consciousness since she was young. At that time, Ayesha still had no idea about what her future career might be. However, she had already developed a fondness for farm life and the countryside, often spending holidays picnicking and roaming outdoors. These were early signs that she would be drawn towards a career connected with villages and farms.

Interestingly, in her childhood, Ayesha had been an inveterate tomboy (always in pants, no makeup, playing with boys); she was an ardent lover of animals (each cow on the farm was addressed by its name); moreover, she always was a mali at heart (took pride in doing all the manual farm jobs herself), and she was gifted with an agile grasshopper mind (jumping easily from one new creative idea to another, like planning and implementing various organic food projects simultaneously).

Ayesha studied at various schools in Mumbai and Delhi and then went on to study in the US. Her elder sister had studied there, and during her visits there, Ayesha became impressed with the liberal atmosphere. She did her undergraduate studies in economics and international government at the Franklin Marshall College, Pennsylvania, and attained her masters degree in global finance at the Graduate School of International Studies, University of Denver. After completing her studies in 1998, she worked for two years in New York with National Economic Research Associates—a private consulting firm. However, she did not expect that work to become her career. She says that her main concern, career wise, in those days was just to have a job that would enable her to pay the bills of living in New York—nothing more idealistic!

In the year 2000, Ayesha started to plan for her return to India. She thought she would set up a small consulting firm to assist Americans who wanted to invest in India and needed help in coping with local issues, as well as set up some dotcom ventures. When she checked out these possibilities with knowledgeable people on her return to

India, it became evident that these plans were not workable because she lacked appropriate experience, and so they were dropped.

Ayesha eventually got a job in Delhi where she was responsible for managing the finance portfolio at Winrock International India, an NGO that encouraged use of renewable energy. The work included designing and managing a USAID programme, which provided low-cost loans and incubation services to projects using renewable energy. Incidentally, the way she got this assignment is interesting and illustrates Ayesha's unconventional and adventurous approach to decision making: Soon after arriving in India, Ayesha had her CV forwarded to potential employers. She received an interview call from Winrock on a Monday, was interviewed on Wednesday, was appointed on Thursday, reported for work on Friday and by that weekend she was off on an extended tour on company work! The person at Winrock who interviewed Ayesha was John Ryan, internationally acclaimed for promoting renewable energy projects in developing countries as well as for his passionate devotion to creating environmentally stable livelihoods for rural communities. At the interview, Ayesha told John that she had no prior experience or knowledge about renewable energy. He replied that he considered her lack of preconceived ideas as a plus point and offered her the job! As it happened, the two of them were destined later to spend many years working closely together in many organizations and on many projects in various parts of the world.

Ayesha left Winrock in 2002 to found a consulting company, Environment, Energy and Enterprise Ventures (E3V), in partnership with John Ryan. E3V undertook assignments related to sustainable rural energy and organic agriculture in India as well as in China, Brazil and the Caribbean. These assignments included projects like the development of micro hydro-based energy generation for organic tea gardens in Darjeeling, the conversion of cow dung into an energy source in China and establishing solar drying systems in Brazil. The projects were enabled through funding from philanthropic US-based organizations that had followed and been impressed by E3V's work.

At this time, Ayesha also founded an organic fruit processing company: Kurmanchal Organic Ventures, which sourced organically grown fruit from the Kumaon hills in Uttarakhand and processed it into products that it then sold in urban markets like the National Capital Region. Also at about this time, Ayesha finally firmed up her thinking about what she would like to do in life as a career: She decided that she would like to spend her life working to improve the lives of small low-income hill farmers by helping them upgrade their activities, particularly through organic ecologically sustainable farming. It turned out that her aspiration became a prophecy of things to come.

As Ayesha approached her mid-1930s, she began to lose interest in the consulting side of her work because it did not satisfy her need to implement projects up to fruition. She explains: 'I wanted to work on projects where I would be directly involved from start to finish and not merely give advice.' She then decided to concentrate on building up TAS, which would fulfil her need to be fully involved in all aspects of hands-on grassroots-level work in the area of sustainable production and marketing of organic foods. By then, her organic fruits firm, Kurmanchal Organic Ventures, was doing well. It had initially focused on apples, but since the apple season is short, plums, peaches, pears and apricots were added to be processed into juices, syrups, jams and chutneys The associate farmers, however, wanted help to sell their other organic products as well, and since TAS was the right organization to do this, Ayesha was further encouraged to devote her time to developing TAS.

Establishing TAS

TAS started in 2009 as an online business. A year later, it also created a few brick-and-mortar shops in urban areas and sold a variety of organic products sourced from Uttarakhand as well as other parts of India, some under the TAS brand and others under the names of producers.

TAS helped hill farmers to upgrade their products and sell them in new markets. For example, if the farmers were growing green bell peppers (*simla mirch*), they were taught to move up the value chain and grow yellow and red bell peppers and thus raise the realization per kilogram from about ₹25 to about ₹250 since TAS would sell their produce to prosperous urban customers who appreciated such things. Similarly, if they were growing cauliflower, they were taught to grow broccoli. Generally, they were encouraged to grow higher-value vegetables which they had not earlier produced because of lack of nearby customers as well as lack of technical and financial resources.

TAS also arranged loans for its associate farmers to build the required greenhouses. These loans were funded by donations from William Grant & Sons, the Scottish whisky makers who were then celebrating the anniversary of their premium single malt whisky—Glenffidich. The donations were through auctions of a limited edition of 11 exclusively aged and numbered bottles of the whisky. Each of these bottles was sold to the highest philanthropic bidder, and the proceeds were donated for projects that benefitted the society in important ways. Ayesha made the presentation to William Grant and was awarded a donation for the TAS greenhouses. The donation was through the Rural & Agricultural Developmental Foundation, an NGO founded by Ayesha and her parents for promoting organic agriculture.

TAS bought the entire produce of the greenhouses, sold it in urban markets and paid good prices to the farmers (after deducting 10 per cent for repayment of loans). Two of TAS' associate farmers used the loans to build greenhouses, and TAS itself built one greenhouse for its own use as a developmental laboratory to experiment with growing ultra-sophisticated imported vegetables such as butternut squash and jalapeño peppers and then passed on the know-how to associate farmers.

TAS tries to exclude middlemen and, for example, buys wheat directly from farmers. Since the wheat needs to be stored, TAS would arrange that a group of farmers gets a loan to create a storage facility. Over time, as TAS buys wheat, the loan is repaid. In the next stage, TAS would arrange a loan for the farmers to establish a flour mill and sell packaged flour instead of wheat. In this way, TAS saves on intermediary costs and could sell value-added organic produce in urban markets at prices that gave good returns to the farmers.

Ayesha had planned that TAS would initially focus on dried herbs, pulses and rice, but soon, because of word-of-mouth publicity, a greater demand was generated. Products handled by TAS soon included meats, dairy products, fruit, vegetables, culinary oils, wholegrain cereals, lentils, spices, herbs, breads and spreads as well as some toiletries such as beeswax lip balm and hand-rolled soap, all made without hazardous chemicals so that they were good for those who consumed them as well as for those who made them.

In 2008, Ayesha was honoured by the Global Environmental Institute, Virginia, the USA, and appointed its first fellow. This fellowship was awarded for her work to create artisanal organic food products as well as to support her activities to help small-scale low-income organic farmers become commercially viable. Under this fellowship, Ayesha did a 10-week professional development programme with Cowgirl Creamery, California, one of America's eminent organic cheese-making establishments. Cowgirl was enthused with Ayesha's mission and generously provided technical assistance. An expert from Cowgirl, the cofounder, travelled to India to guide Ayesha in the development of artisan cheese-making businesses. Under this fellowship, Ayesha also received support to conduct research in other organic food products, particularly the basic principles of their preparation that she could later adapt to local conditions.

Challenges

As the founder of TAS, Ayesha had to overcome several challenges before she could get her business up and running:

Finance

Ayesha started TAS with a capital of ₹40 lakhs—saved from her earlier consultancy income. But TAS required a much larger infusion of funds to buy merchandize up front as well as to finance value-added services like storage, processing and packaging. The start-up was tough. All costs had to be tightly controlled to conserve funds. This tight control over expenses resulted in austere working conditions. For example, inventory was often stored in Ayesha's living quarters, sometimes under her bed! Also her home was treated as a dormitory where visiting associate farmers from Uttarakhand were put up. At that time, Ayesha was still also working for E3V, and she used that salary to meet some of TAS' expenses.

As in the case of many other women's entrepreneurial ventures, access to institutional finance was not easy. Fortunately, because of her education and experience, Ayesha knew the 'tricks of the trade' with respect to raising funds from financial institutions. However, she preferred that most of the funding for her projects was through equity raised from family and friends. She avoided bank loans because of the pressure of fixed payments with deadlines.

TAS' annual sales in 2014 were around ₹3.5 crores. At this level of business, the generation of funds was adequate to cover current operating expenses and provide for normal growth, as well as cover a modest salary for Ayesha.

POSITIONING

Reducing the influence of middlemen (*aarat*s) in the rural supply chain was a major challenge. To overcome the dependency of the farmer on the *aarat*, TAS too had to be present for the farmer for the whole time and provide help in times of sickness, crop failure, weddings, and so forth. So Ayesha arranged the permanent presence of

TAS in the hill areas of Uttarakhand. This also resulted in more direct buying from farmers, a key TAS objective.

Also Ayesha had to build trust and convince people about the reliability, integrity and intentions of TAS. Buyers often cannot differentiate between organic and artificially grown produce. TAS labeled its products as 'organic' or as 'natural'. Any produce that was certified under the guidelines of the Agricultural and Processed Food Products Export Development Authority (APEDA) as meeting international organic specifications was labelled 'organic'. The Uttarakhand government helped farmers get this certification, but many farmers found the certification costs too high. TAS also distributed products that were not certified under APEDA guidelines but were nevertheless grown under organic conditions—these products were labelled as 'natural'. This transparency in labelling worked well and fairly. TAS soon became a trusted name in the organic food retail business.

HUMAN RESOURCES

Another problem Ayesha faced was in the area of HR, particularly attracting top-grade professional talent to work in remote hill areas. For example, she had difficulty finding a CEO for TAS who could take care of all operational matters so that she herself could focus on new product development—her main strength. As it is she travelled extensively, visited food fairs all over the world and interacted with leaders in the organic foods business in the international meeting places of such people like the Borough Market in London. She knew how to search out new sophisticated organic products, research their adaptability to Indian conditions and then arrange for the technologies to be transferred to TAS' associates. She felt she could contribute most by devoting her time to such activities if she could be relieved from operational work by a competent CEO. She is still trying to deal with this problem.

CULTURAL ISSUES

In India, girls are often dissuaded from starting businesses because they are expected to devote their time to family and home. Ayesha did not have to face such pressures. Her parents were broadminded and fully supportive of her entrepreneurial endeavours although they did sometimes gently suggest to her that she could consider the benefits of family life and even introduced her to some 'suitable' boys. In fact, Ayesha was able to establish and run her enterprises without feeling pressurized to get married. In 2013, Ayesha turned 40 and was happily unmarried. She was very active, successful in her work, full of life, vivacious and in good health (the organic food!). Incidentally, to a great extent, her niece and nephew fulfilled her maternal needs. Ayesha knew that she could have a happy fulfilling life in her chosen area of work, and she did not feel the need for any ties. She decided, and even announced, that she would not get married. There was no question of any objection from the family.

Ayesha says that throughout her entrepreneurial career, she did not face sociocultural challenges on account of being a woman. Her most significant contacts were with small farmers in hill areas, and they were always polite and respectful, although somewhat bemused at the idea of a smart city girl talking to them about village farm issues! But her helpful attitude helped her earn their trust and there was never any friction. Also, with regard to her relationships with village-level bureaucrats and politicians, Ayesha did not encounter problems because most of them did not know how to approach a lady with Ayesha's personality, particularly as at most meetings she happened to be the only female present. Also, it was evident to all of them that she was doing useful work for the local community, particularly for women.

Future

Ayesha has clear and strong ideas about TAS' future. Her intention is not just to make TAS large and prosperous. She would rather see TAS promoting organic food in a way that improves the lives of small, low-income farmers as well as conserves the environment. She says: 'Currently, only 30 per cent of TAS' merchandize comes directly from farmers; I want to increase that substantially.' For Ayesha, these are the relevant measures of success rather than size or profitability. So although TAS does benefit the consumers of organic food, its main concern is benefiting the producers, particularly the small farmers in remote hill areas.

Further, Ayesha would like to see TAS become an organization that continually innovates and diversifies into new artisanal organic foods. She has already made some very beneficial technology transfer arrangements for organic products such as Californian cheeses and Cumberland pork sausages, which are being produced by TAS associates with the know-how supplied by Cowgirl, California, and Silfield Farms, Cumbria. She is now working on a new project to make cider. The New Forest Cider company, an eminent British artisanal cider maker, is providing the know-how.

When asked how she manages to obtain expensive know-how from industry leaders without much payout, Ayesha says: 'Owners of small-scale organic food businesses are, by and large, not greedy people; they are helpful and keen that their work flourishes. Convincing these people to help build capabilities in India is not difficult, particularly as this would not pose a threat to them in their existing markets.' There is, of course, also the matter of approaching these people in a tactful way—and in this regard, Ayesha can be quite persuasive!

The way in which Ayesha persuaded New Forest to help her establish a cider project in Uttarakhand is revealing. One day at the Borough Market in London, Ayesha saw the stall of this cider maker. She went over and introduced herself to the lady at the counter and told her about TAS' activities in the faraway Uttarakhand in India. She said she wanted to explore the possibility of New Forest helping her with know-how to establish a cider-making facility there. The lady, Mary Topp, talked to her father, the founder of the business, Barry Topp who became highly enthused with the exciting idea. Ayesha then explained to them that TAS was not in a position to pay any fancy know-how fees, no matter how well deserved. She said she could only afford to pay for an air ticket and local hospitality for a technician's visit. Barry readily accepted this cheeky proposal, which had been presented with Ayesha's usual disarmingly frank charm.

Soon Barry, accompanied by Mary, arrived in Uttarakhand to start work on the cider-making project. Ayesha paid for all expenses associated with Barry's travel from England to India. Although she did not pay for the expenses associated with Mary's travel, she did pay for local hospitality in India for both Barry and Mary.

Incidentally, their stay in Uttarakhand was at the Sitla resort of Vikram Maira, another avid protagonist of sustainable rural development, so the accommodation charges were generously discounted.

Barry also took Ayesha around to meet other organic food producers who made products that could be appropriate for TAS. He introduced her to Peter Gott, the founder of Silfield Farms, Cumbria, the acclaimed makers of organic pork sausages. Peter told Ayesha all about making organic, gluten-free pork sausages, and these were soon being made by TAS associates in India and sold through its outlets.

TAS's entry into new products is generating a lot of activity. For example, in cheese making, there are issues such as the transportation of milk from the cattle farms to the cheese-making facility requiring expensive refrigeration, as well as questions about the types of cheese that would be appropriate for the Indian market—these matters are being researched. Similarly, there are matters concerning organic pork sausages. The cider project will throw up its own issues, possibly concerned with regulations. All this will keep Ayesha and the TAS team busy for a long time. One needs to appreciate that each of these projects has been more than a lifetime's work for the leaders in the field, be it Cowgirl in California, Silfield Farms in Cumbria or the cider maker in New Forest.

The new projects have given Ayesha confidence and encouragement to develop more activities related to organic food. She is aware that TAS does not yet have the financial or management resources to implement many of the projects that she has in mind. such as new sophisticated organic products including confectionary, pies, and so on, as well as new business lines such as opening organic food restaurants, catering organic meals as well as some others that are still in the realm of dreams. So she is now doing something that she had avoided doing earlier that is searching for partners who could invest in TAS as well as provide appropriate management support. Such strategic investors will not be easy to find because they would need to be people who share Ayesha's values and philosophy. However, given her record in handling such matters, this may not take too long!

Gyan about Organic Foods

What is the main advantage of organic food? Less pesticide, less harmful chemicals.

Is organic food more expensive? Yes! Because of production costs. Incidentally, the lower prices of conventionally grown food do not reflect the costs of environmental degradation and damage to health, particularly of children. The prices of organically grown food reflect the truer cost to society, particularly with respect to staples like grains and lentils. Regarding masalas, the organic stuff is stronger, so less is required and works out cheaper.

What about meats and eggs? These are healthier and tastier if the livestock is not confined in cages. Also, it is more humane to let livestock roam.

(One should also think about lower spends on vitamin supplements and doctor's fees!)

If one can afford only a little organic food, which items would you suggest? Go for the fruit and veggies because the conventional alternatives absorb more pesticides.

7

Saloni Malhotra

Rural BPO

Saloni Malhotra, a passionate advocate for creating skilled jobs in rural areas, is the founder of DesiCrew, a socially motivated business process outsourcing (BPO) company that provides IT-enabled services from its delivery centres established in villages. She is acclaimed for training young rural people in computer operations and then employing them for outsourced work, which would otherwise not have been available to them unless they migrated to cities. DesiCrew initially offered basic low-end services and then gradually upgraded itself to supplying sophisticated high-end e-commerce and analytical services. DesiCrew prides itself in generating wealth in rural areas rather than extracting wealth from rural areas. As this pattern of inclusive growth is replicated at the national level, there would be a significant impact on the rural economy.

Background

Saloni grew up in South Delhi and went to school at the Carmel Convent. Her parents are doctors. Her mother is a consultant gynaecologist with a private practice and her father recently retired as professor and head of the Department of Nuclear Medicine at the prestigious All India Institute of Medical Sciences. Saloni, however, decided to tread her own path and took to studying engineering.

Her parents encouraged Saloni to pursue her mission of creating skilled jobs in rural areas and helped her overcome some of the challenges that hinder young Indian girls from starting a business away from home. For example, there was never any pressure from the parents on Saloni to give priority to marriage and family life. In fact, they often told Saloni that she must first establish herself in a career and only then think of marriage. She followed their advice and devoted her time and efforts to building DesiCrew. In fact, the work at DesiCrew was so hectic that there was no way that she could have found time to look at marriage possibilities.

Saloni says: 'My desire to work in rural India was reconfirmed at the engineering college when one of my colleagues at the college, Pallavi, from rural Maharashtra,
one day proudly told me, she was going to study Computer
Sciences. Later, I learnt that the poor girl had very little
access to a computer. She just believed that studying
Computer Sciences would help her get a well-paid job and
the benefits which follow. I felt very bad for people like
her who live in rural areas and miss out on opportunities
which city people take for granted. Pallavi made me realize that she and I had one thing in common; we lacked
exposure to each other's worlds. It struck me that when
we think of livelihood options for youngsters in rural
areas we think of agriculture or handicrafts and ignore
opportunities in high-tech areas. Young graduates from
arts, commerce and engineering flock to cities to find jobs
in high tech areas. Could we not move the jobs to these
people, rather than move these people to jobs in large
cities? I became enthused with the idea of creating tech-
nologically advanced employment for educated rural
youngsters in their villages. In fact it became my mission.'

At the engineering college in Pune, Saloni took a keen
interest in extracurricular activities. She was President of
the junior wing of the Lions Club, which was involved in
many developmental activities in villages around Pune.
This experience made her realize that she would enjoy,
and be good at, developmental work in rural areas.

Saloni decided that after her engineering studies, she
would not like to follow the usual path of doing an MBA
and preferred instead to gain some work experience
before taking any decision about a career. Her first job
was with a start-up called WebChutney, a leading interac-
tive Web solutions consultancy in Delhi. Her intention

then was to learn about managing a start-up. At that time, she was still considering what she would eventually like to do in her working life.

Although Saloni wanted to work for the upliftment of rural youngsters, she did not want to do charity. She wanted to start her own profit-making business, which would create skilled jobs in villages. She then happened to meet with Professor Ashok Jhunjhunwala of IIT Chennai who had earlier incubated the TeNet Group, a telecom venture that created broadband networks in rural areas to spread world-class technology at affordable prices. He was also known for promoting the idea of social businesses that would infuse money into rural areas—all this greatly appealed to Saloni. The professor was in Delhi giving a lecture sharing his experiences. Later, he also spoke about the large number of jobs that the BPO industry had created in urban India. He posed the question: 'Why not in rural India, too?' Among his audience was Saloni, then a 23-year-old recently qualified engineer who desperately wanted to work in rural India. She was inspired by the professor and wrote to him asking for an opportunity to work with him. Initially, the professor was not sure whether she was serious, but she persisted. Impressed by her perseverance, the professor asked her to meet him at the Rural Technology & Business Incubation Centre at IIT Chennai.

When Saloni arrived in Chennai a couple of days later, the professor quizzed her comprehensively about her intentions and plans. At that time, ideas about what exactly she would like to do had not yet crystallized in Saloni's mind. The interview with Professor Jhunjhunwala helped sort out her ideas. She got attracted to the idea of starting an outsourcing business that combined a rural workforce with modern communication technology. Professor Jhunjhunwala felt that the project should be implemented and that IIT Chennai would take on Saloni's project for incubation. This would provide Saloni with initial seed funding, office space and basic infrastructure as well as mentoring and contacts.

Saloni had undertaken the trip to Chennai planning to stay for one or two days, but after her interview with Professor Jhunjhunwalla, she just stayed put for seven years!

Saloni quit her job in Delhi in 2004 and relocated to Chennai to commence the incubation. Language was a major problem as also were other social issues like understanding the local culture and inspiring rural youngsters to share her vision. All this involved hard work but was successfully managed mainly because of the drive of a young girl's missionary zeal to realize her dream. Saloni received support from IIT Chennai and from helpful local people. On the personal front, she lived with Dr Rajaram and his wife Lalitha, who were also interested in rural development. They took care of her as would her own parents. They shared a similar interest in rural development, and Saloni became a founding trustee in their foundation for rural development.

About starting work on the project, Saloni says: 'Professor Jhunjhunwala wanted us to create employment and infuse income into rural areas by creating many small BPOs in villages staffed by local residents, initially in Tamil Nadu and Karnataka. I was given eighteen months to implement the project and start the BPO company. First I spent time understanding the local culture. Then I checked out different kinds of locations to understand where we could base our activities and also checked out the various kinds of models for developing rural BPOs as a business. For example I checked out whether DesiCrew could work through the many Internet kiosks, which already existed in Tamil Nadu and Karnataka for promoting education in villages. However that idea was dropped because it involved dealing with the long periods of time when the computers in the kiosks were not utilized, making this model uneconomical. Similarly the idea of getting villagers to work from their homes was considered a non-starter because of inadequate infrastructure and lack of understanding of the BPO business requirements. Saloni noticed that village people lacked adequate facilities at home and also lacked the discipline to voluntarily work long regular hours.'

Other business models were then also considered. Working through franchisees was one such model. However, Saloni discovered that franchisees were not interested in investing to grow the business. They looked for quick returns up front. They often bought cheap second-hand computers that got viruses and created problems. For getting business, Saloni had to approach friends and contacts from IIT—some work did materialize but was not sufficient to feed a business and certainly not scalable. One unscrupulous franchisee walked away with the business that DesiCrew had generated and the entire trained team as well as all the equipment! Saloni had to approach the police for redressal. Within three months, Saloni realized that the franchisee model would not work.

Meanwhile, time was running out, and Saloni had to get back to Prof. Jhunjhunwalla with a workable business within the stipulated period. Pressure was building up. It then became evident to Saloni that the business model that could work for DesiCrew was to establish and manage its own BPO centres. She then focused on defining the

DesiCrew Business Model. To begin with, she planned to buy out some franchisees and convert their centres into company-owned establishments, with DesiCrew making the required extra investment.

Saloni recalls: 'Many names for the new company were suggested. DesiCrew was considered best: "Desi" means native and "crew" means workforce: short and apt!' DesiCrew started work in January 2005 and was registered after the incubation period as a private limited company in February 2007.

The DesiCrew Business Model

DesiCrew's technology-driven, profit-making social enterprise provides competitive outsourcing solutions for clients as well as upmarket employment opportunities for rural youngsters who are trained and then employed in their own villages, thus enabling them to save about 90 per cent of their income as opposed to only about 10 per cent if they moved to a city.

Urban BPOs often hire youngsters from rural areas who then have to migrate to cities. DesiCrew instead moves the jobs to the villagers. This encourages them to stay rural and discourages rural-to-urban migration. The DesiCrew model also helps the Indian BPO industry overcome two of its major problems: ever-increasing real estate costs and high rates of attrition.

DesiCrew's first set of rural BPOs were established in Bhavani, Mayiladhurai and Tirupur, which are villages close to Chennai and Coimbatore. Its most recent centre is located in the coastal village of Kaup in the Western Ghats of Karnataka.

A publishing house named New Horizon Media gave DesiCrew its first outsourcing assignment. This involved producing digitalized versions of books. Badri Seshadri, the company's director, said: 'The job was well done, it cost less, it generated skilled employment in rural areas which is a good thing; and there was no delay in getting back the digitalized books since the work was online.'

To begin with, DesiCrew provided basic BPO services such as data entry, conversion, digitization, updating databases and transcription involving English and Indian languages. Later, DesiCrew's performance showed that its rural BPOs were capable of more than mere basic low-end work. In December 2007, two major organizations provided breakthroughs for DesiCrew: HDFC Standard Life and Google India R&D. HDFC's assignment involved tracking and arranging insurance applications; Google's assignment involved incorporating details into GPS-based maps. Both assignments required work that prompted DesiCrew into becoming a company that offered new sophisticated services to reputed companies. Such services included content scanning and cleaning, secondary research and management logistics. DesiCrew then began to offer high-end services across various verticals—marketing, finance, media, e-governance, and the social sector to various clients, including publishers, banks, and hospitals insurance companies, in India and abroad.

By the end of 2007, though the company was still struggling, its future appeared promising, and some large BPOs as well as investors offered to buy the company on attractive terms. However, DesiCrew's dedicated and well-knit core team was concerned that new owners may alter the mission of the company. Saloni discussed the proposals with her core team and then indicated the alternatives—either DesiCrew sells or sweats it out possibly with salary cuts. The team strongly recommended that DesiCrew should not sell and should continue its focus on providing technical employment to educated youngsters in their villages, which was the ideal that had inspired them. So the offers to buy out DesiCrew were turned down.

At this time, Rajiv Kuchhal, a mentor to Saloni, decided to invest in DesiCrew as an angel investor. Rajiv had led Infosys' BPO and brought with him immense experience and knowledge of the sector. He came on board in July 2008 and provided substantial momentum to DesiCrew.

DesiCrew got a particularly challenging assignment from the Infrastructure Leasing and Finance Corporation, which was working with the Government of Rajasthan. The assignment involved reaching out to millions of poor female beneficiaries of a state government welfare programme, registering their details and enabling the opening of bank accounts for each beneficiary to facilitate direct transfer of monetary benefits. This was a huge project, which stretched DesiCrew's capabilities to its limits. DesiCrew set up a new office in Jaipur and moved four of its key executives there. The idea was to bring back work to the existing DesiCrew centres. However, when the project commenced, the project brief changed and the scope of work increased substantially from a manpower requirement of 300 to a requirement of 15,000. DesiCrew was confronted with a dilemma. The company had to quickly think of innovative ways of executing this project. The new Jaipur office was converted into a project management office, and the team of four then quickly hired small data processing operators and computer centres across the length and breadth of Rajasthan and began farming out work to people across the state. As a result of this project, DesiCrew developed in-house capabilities to handle e-government work on a massive scale.

The Organization for Economic Co-operation and Development estimates that there are about 130 million educated people in rural India with little access to meaningful employment. DesiCrew plans to leverage this potential. In 2013, it had five rural delivery centres in Tamil Nadu and Karnataka. In the next two to three years, it planned to have 10–15 centres across India, each employing about a hundred people. Saloni explained: 'We wanted to substantially increase the number of people we train and employ in villages and also we wanted a pan-India presence because there was a growing demand for skills in Indian languages. Also, we wanted to continually climb up the value chain with respect to our service offerings.'

Most employees at DesiCrew's rural delivery centres are girls as boys have the option to move to find work, whereas the girls have to stay back till they get married. As these girls earn well, their self-esteem grows. This also encourages parents to support a daughter's education, which is a desirable outcome. Often, after a centre has existed in a village for about three years, boys also begin opting to stay back in their village to work with DesiCrew. When this happened, it was like a litmus test that indicated that DesiCrew had then established a lasting presence in that village.

Challenges

Starting DesiCrew was a unique and novel venture that involved overcoming many challenges, as discussed in the subsequent sections.

The first problem faced in setting up rural BPOs was finding suitable staff in unfamiliar villages. The project needed youngsters with a minimum qualification of 12th class as well as some basic knowledge of computers. To overcome the problem of finding staff, DesiCrew worked closely with a local entrepreneur who had good connections in the village. After this entrepreneur had identified suitable candidates, their CVs were appraised and short-listed candidates took online tests; this was followed by interviews conducted by DesiCrew executives. DesiCrew ran a programme called D-Touch, which trained youngsters for three months and then provided internships to promising candidates. In this way, DesiCrew was able to find sufficient employable staff for its centres in villages.

The next problem was training the selected staff in their village. As most recruits were first-generation workers in a corporate set-up, an orientation session was required. The rural staff was hardworking and sincere and had a strong desire to learn, but they lacked fluency in communication. At DesiCrew, apart from project-specific training, continuous coaching was provided in language, Internet and email usage and other soft skills. In addition, certain positive attitudes were instilled into its employees such as determination to surpass customer's expectations and to always work ethically and with optimum utilization of resources.

Another challenge was to create adequate facilities to change the perception that rural BPOs may not deliver efficiently. Saloni says: 'DesiCrew invested heavily in infrastructure—to ensure that there was no downtime due to power, connectivity or equipment failure. All offices and centres had generators, UPS and backups. DesiCrew's engineers created two new Web-based applications—Click2.0 and ICT Pegasus, which enabled rural staff to work on BPO jobs from distant locations and helped DesiCrew manage its remote workforce. These applications helped to check and improve quality so that errors were caught and fixed before delivery. For example, in Pegasus, a document was split into small forms and two unrelated operators filled each form; in case of a mismatch, the form was sent to a third operator for checking. Customers who took time to visit DesiCrew centres were impressed and always gave us business when they saw our facilities.'

An important task was to find and persuade new customers in India and abroad to outsource work to DesiCrew's rural centres. This required strenuous marketing efforts to explain how the customer got quality work at prices that were competitive because of low living costs, rent, transportation and absence of attrition.

With regard to funding, Saloni had received initial seed money as part of the incubation from IIT Chennai, and she also invested some of her personal savings. The business also generated some money. Incidentally, in the initial days of bootstrapping, DesiCrew funded its business through winning small amounts of money as prizes in Business Plan competitions!

The economics of the rural BPO business has some distinctive features, which make it difficult to manage financially. Most BPO clients are very cost conscious and are unwilling to pay a fee that exceeds their preconceived idea of an appropriate individual per diem for a rural centre. Often, their preconceived idea of an appropriate individual per diem is too low for DesiCrew centres, which pay well and maintain high standards of service. Managing cash flows was always a tricky balancing act, and Saloni often faced much stress making ends meet.

Saloni voiced her views about socio-cultural challenges faced by women entrepreneurs because of their sex: 'These challenges are mostly in the mind. It did not occur to me to think about such issues. In my experience, my age rather than my gender created difficulties. Because I was young and inexperienced, people would not take me seriously, and I found it difficult to build trust. In fact some business people dealt with me as if I was collecting material for a thesis!'

This was not surprising, because Saloni is youthful, petite and looks young for her age. When asked if male executives sometimes tried to make passes or improper advances, Saloni said: 'It is common, so there is no point in making an issue about it; moreover, it is easily handled.'

About Saloni's own experience with entrepreneurship, she says: 'Working on an idea from scratch with no handbook to follow was both challenging and fun! Also I love to travel and I wanted to start something like DesiCrew to travel to remote areas. I guess it comes down to taking risks. Incidentally, being an entrepreneur has been glorified very much. Let's not forget that at the end of the day, one is only as good as one's team. My suggestion to entrepreneurs establishing a start-up is that they must have the will to persevere and the dedication to put in long hours of very hard work.'

The Future

The Indian BPO industry as well as DesiCrew grew substantially in the five years between 2007 and 2012. This spectacular growth created a peculiar problem for DesiCrew: Saloni began to feel that DesiCrew was being left behind. Her target had been to create over 1,000 jobs, but DesiCrew had only achieved about one-third of that number. Saloni was concerned that DesiCrew was not growing at a rapid pace because of her leadership. She said, 'I realized that there are different kinds of leaders— some who enjoy building from scratch, some who like taking things to the next level and some who like to fix broken companies. I am the first kind. I love to start things.' Saloni felt that DesiCrew needed a more mature and experienced leadership to grow at the pace it deserved. She had enjoyed the chaos of a business start-up but did not look forward to running an established business. She felt that the time had come for her to leave the management of DesiCrew to an appropriate kind of leader and for her to find new avenues that excited her more.

As a matter of fact, Saloni had done excellent work by getting DesiCrew up and running. She had put in place a powerful management team that included experienced and knowledgeable people who after studying at some of the best universities in the world went on to hold senior positions in global companies such as Tata, Siemens and Infosys as well as in developmental organizations. Also at the staff level, DesiCrew had people with ITI diplomas, degrees and even postgraduate qualifications. Interns from the US and other countries would apply to work with DesiCrew, and their case studies were then circulated in top B-schools. All these people had been attracted to work in DesiCrew because of its mission and values. Apart from building a strong and dedicated organization, Saloni had upgraded the services offered by DesiCrew and expanded its list of clients to include many highly respected private and public organizations from India and abroad. Moreover, DesiCrew had become a profitable company. In spite of these achievements, Saloni continued to feel that the time had come for her to leave DesiCrew. She did, of course, realize that business process outsourcing was a capital-intensive business and needed deep pockets, whereas she had come into the business with no capital; in fact, she had set out to create an ambitious project without the necessary wherewithal!

By the end of 2010, Saloni conveyed to the DesiCrew Board that a new CEO should be appointed and that she would step down, after arranging a substantial funding to provide DesiCrew with a boost. Saloni brought on board VenturEast, an equity fund investor that made a substantial investment in DesiCrew. She then quit as CEO of DesiCrew, although she continued to serve on its Board as a Director.

When asked about her experience of leaving the company she built, she explains: 'I felt I needed to step back and look at things from different perspectives. Perhaps I was not providing all the inputs required to make DesiCrew realize its full potential and perhaps it would be better for DesiCrew to have a new set of professionals at the helm. Even though I initiated my exit, it wasn't easy to step down. Paul Basil, Founder CEO of Villgro at the Lemelson Foundation, was my personal mentor through this experience, and without his support, I would have not been able to make a smooth and positive exit.'

For all the years spent building DesiCrew and working 18+ hours a day, Saloni took a year off to enjoy herself. She travelled to new places, learnt scuba diving, cooking and meditation amongst other things. She also got a scholarship to attend a management programme in Sweden on *Social Innovation in the Digital Context*, which dealt with how human rights issues could be resolved on the

Internet. She got involved in establishing Safecity, creating a safer environment for women. Safecity is a platform that encourages women to share their personal stories of sexual harassment in public places in India. At Safecity, data gets aggregated as hot spots on maps indicating danger levels at various places. These maps are useful for individuals, local communities and the civil administration. Safecity was runner-up for the Facebook 2014 Social Innovation Award and was nominated for the Google Business Award. Safecity is catching traction with the law enforcement agencies as well as civil society to make public spaces safe.

Saloni has a large part of her working life ahead of her. She is a positive person, and from her past record, it is evident that she will continue to strive to benefit society and the environment with positive change. She continues to be on the Board of DesiCrew and contributes to strategic decision making at the organization. Further, she has devoted time to the formulation of the National Rural BPO Policy, which the Ministry of Information Technology and Communications brought out recently. She has also become an advisor to some innovative organizations such as SevaMob, a low-cost insurance provider; StartUp!, a social enterprise incubator, and Traveller Kids, an edutainment company for kids.

What others see as a problem, Saloni sees as an opportunity. When others complain that something needs to be done, Saloni will act—not wait for 'somebody to do something'.

8

Binalakshmi Nepram

NGO for Widowed Women

The sun was setting over the village of Wabgai Lamkhai in the hills of Thoubal district of Manipur on 24 December 2004, when three armed men entered the car battery repair shop of 27-year-old Buddhi Moirangthem and forcibly dragged him out onto the road. As he struggled, the assailants shot him dead. The brazen execution was done in minutes, out in the open with no attempt at concealment. There happened to be a young girl present near the scene of this brutal act: Binalakshmi Nepram, a Manipuri research student, was carrying out a study in the area. This awful incident changed her life completely. She decided then that she would work to help women who became widows because of the rampant violence in her home state, and she immediately set about this work with determination and courage.

Beautiful Manipur lies in the northeast corner of India and is bounded by Nagaland in the north, Mizoram in the south and Assam in the west, and it shares an international border with Upper Myanmar in the east. It is blessed with exquisite natural scenery and exotic flora flourishing in a land full of streams; lotus, lavender and lilac lakes; silvery waterfalls and luxuriant forests. It is surrounded by the misty blue-green hills of the Lower Himalayas. Manipur is also rich in culture and traditions as depicted in its exquisite handicrafts as well as its many colourful festivals.

But Manipur is also India's most conflict-ridden state. It has had a long history of brutal violence from the time that the Maharaja of the ancient kingdom of Manipur signed the instrument of accession to join the Indian Union in 1949. That act of accession let loose formidable waves of militancy resulting from competing political demands, struggles over natural resources, illegal migration, displacement and exclusion by various ethnic groups as well as by governmental armed forces and security personnel. Over twenty thousand people have been killed in the past five decades, mainly young men in the age group of 19–42 years, resulting in a large number of widows—the gun survivors.

The Manipur Women Gun Survivors Network

Binalakshmi established The Manipur Women Gun Survivors Network to help women like the young wife of Budhi Moirangthem, who was suddenly widowed following the brutal attack on her husband on Christmas eve in 2004. Binalakshmi arranged a donation of ₹4,500 to buy her a sewing machine. This was the very first intervention by the network, and it enabled the widow, Rebika, to stitch together the torn remnants of her life.

The network helps victims of armed violence whose lives have been shattered because of the killing of a husband, a father, a brother or a son; women and children suffer the most in this conflict as they bear the brunt of its emotional and socioeconomic shock. The assistance provided by the network is multipronged: The immediate needs of the bereaved woman are food and continuation of children's education. The network addresses these needs and also helps create sustainable income streams by arranging for the widows to start small businesses. The widows are helped to open their own bank accounts and also provided with interest-free microfinance so that they can start small selling or production activities like weaving, silk reeling, growing mushrooms and rearing poultry, pigs, fish and so on. For example, in the case of Huidrom Tanya, whose father was gunned down when she was 18, the network arranged a loan of ₹3,000 with which she was able to start a small vending business, selling daily needs in the streets. As time passed, her confidence grew and she later became the proud owner of a small shop that sold embroidered dress materials, incense sticks and household goods. Then there was the case of Mumtaz, whose lecturer husband was killed by unidentified gunmen. She was in great distress as she had to care for five children. The network arranged ₹8,000 to help her with her handloom unit. Her success as a businesswoman instilled confidence in her, and she now plans to contest the local panchayat elections so that she could bring about improvements in her village. There are dozens of such cases where widows have been helped by the network to start income-earning businesses.

The network also provides legal assistance to women to fight their cases for justice since they cannot afford lawyers. Medical assistance is made available, which takes care of their health needs through arrangements with philanthropic hospitals and doctors who are willing to provide free check-ups, dental care and so on. Professional psychologists are engaged to counsel the women to overcome trauma. The Manipur Women Gun Survivors Network is the first initiative of its kind in India. The network is apolitical, although Binalakshmi has often been wrongly accused of having political ambitions. Politicians, in any case, have generally stayed away from organizations like this network, which is probably a good thing for all concerned.

Binalakshmi's Background

Binalakshmi is a civil rights activist who is spearheading work on caring for victims of armed conflict as well as work on women-led disarmament. She has written extensively on militancy, small arms proliferation and women's roles in peace building. She is also author of four books: *Poetic Festoon* (1990), *Armed Conflict, Narcotics and Small Arms Proliferation in India's Northeast* (2002) and *Meckley* (2004), as well as an edited volume *India and the Arms Trade Treaty* (2009). Incidentally, the novel *Meckley* was a comprehensive personal sociocultural exploration of Manipur. Earlier, she published a journal called *Borderlines*, which looked at wars and insurgencies in India's northeast and ways of bringing peace to the region.

Binalakshmi received recognition from various national and international organizations, She was invited to lecture at the Asia Pacific Centre for Security Studies in Hawaii; she was awarded the WISCOMP Peace Award by the Foundation of Universal Responsibility of His Holiness the Dalai Lama and she was awarded the Sean MacBride Peace Prize, the CNN IBN Real Heroes Award and Indian of the Year Award. She was also awarded the Ploughshares and the Ashoka Fellowships. The London-based Action on Armed Violence named Binalakshmi among the 100 most influential people in the world working on armed violence reduction. While pursuing her studies, she also attended the United Nations Review Conference on Small Arms and Light Weapons in New York and a meeting of the Nobel Prize–winning International Pugwash Society in Nova Scotia.

Binalakshmi was born in Imphal in 1974 and witnessed massacres, armed conflict and curfews throughout her childhood. These incidents had come to be regarded as the normal way of life in Manipur. In fact, when Binalakshmi was being born at the District Hospital in Imphal, there was a curfew on (which did not deter her from appearing in this world!).

Binalakshmi grew up in a quaint little Manipuri village called Heirangoithong, and she has recorded memories of the place and its people in her novel *Meckley*. There was a terrible massacre in Heirangoithong in 1984 when 13 civilians were killed allegedly by the Central Reserve Police Force, which is protected by the Armed Forces Special

Powers Act. This event is etched deeply in the memory of the locals and of Binalakshmi. Such happenings gave rise to a remarkably spectacular form of protest called *Meira Paibis* in which crowds of women carrying homemade fire-torches walked in the streets—an awe-inspiring sight! Incidentally, in spite of protests, the hated Armed Forces Special Powers Act is still operational in Manipur. This is a draconian law that was introduced by the British rulers of colonial India to be used against Indian freedom fighters. It confers substantial powers on military personnel to punish, even kill, any number of civilians whom they suspect of disturbing peace.

Binalakshmi's siblings comprised three sisters and three brothers. Her parents gave the children an admirable upbringing with respect to studies as well as extracurricular activities. Binalaksnmi's mother was a zoologist. She retired as principal of an educational academy. She had always been a working mother, and during childhood, Binalakshmi wondered why she was so often absent from home. It was much later that she realized the values of a working mother. Her father was Manipur's Additional Director of Industries, although he was personally more inclined towards literature and the arts. He introduced the children to the joys of reading. Binalakshmi recalls the children's section of the State Central Library where her father and the children spent several pleasant hours browsing and where she also developed an interest in writing. Her father took them to gardens to look at flowers and he also showed them films, some of which were not quite appropriate for their age! Her parents struggled to raise the children to be humane and to do the best for their society. Binalakshmi was later to live her life with commitment to these ideals.

As a schoolgirl in the Little Flower School in Imphal, Binalakshmi was bright, serious and hardworking. She won several prizes in competitions, debates and quizzes and was also the head girl. She completed the High School Leaving Certificate Examination in 1990 and was ranked second in the state, doing very well in Mathematics and English. The family decided to send her for preuniversity studies to the much acclaimed and fashionable Lady Keane College in Shillong in the neighbouring State of Assam. In Shillong, by the age of 18, it was already evident that Binalakshmi would blossom into a lady of consequence. She was devoted to high ideals, was passionate, determined and fiercely independent and was endowed with a kind heart. Physically, she was well-built, strong and graceful. She was attractive, with expressive eyes and shoulder-length straight silken hair framing a dusky oval face with a regal aquiline nose. She did not spend her time in Shillong enjoying outings and dating, like many of the other girls in the college. Binalakshmi greatly missed her home and family. To overcome her grief, she devoted most of her time and energy to her studies and also began writing notes for what would eventually become her novel *Meckley*. She also took to poetry and playing music. She became a member of the hostel committee and fought for improved food—a sign of the combative spirit that would show up often in her later career!

About her grief on being away from home, she then wrote:

It is like being hurled down a slope with no support, and you know that you have no one but yourself as your lone anchor.

After Binalakshmi completed her preuniversity studies in Shillong in 1992, it became evident that she had the potential to make a significant contribution to society and that she should study further. Her father took her to seek admission in the University of Delhi. She gained admission to the Physics Honours course at the much-sought-after Miranda House, but she finally got to join the History Honours course at the less famous but more picturesque Inderprastha College. She took her studies very seriously as well as participated in extracurricular activities. She was secretary, and later president, of the History Society and presented well-researched papers at several seminars.

After graduating in History Honours from Indraprastha College for Women, she got admission in the MA course in History at the prestigious Hindu College of the University of Delhi. She had to live in rented rooms close to the university and earned money to pay for living expenses by giving tuitions. In the torrid heat of Delhi nights, Binalakshmi missed the balmy cool weather of Manipur and she also greatly missed the people at home. To create a feeling of being in touch, she would step out and observe the moon, which she knew would also be shining on her home and on her loved ones; in particular, she knew that her mother often watched the moon. This little ritual of looking at the moon gave her a feeling of connection with home, although she was thousands of miles away.

During her days at the Hindu College, Binalkshmi also got more deeply involved into poetry—she wrote poems, participated in recitals and interacted with India's most respected poets. She also devoted time to arranging her notes, penned over the past few years, into the novel *Meckley*, with text enriched by inputs from her poetical efforts. In a philosophical poem, she wrote:

*History and our present lives Our present lives
and history
Are they related? As time weaves our history;
And history weaves our present lives; We all get
woven—
History and our present lives, Our present lives
and history.*

Life in Delhi was hectic and exhausting. It often involved travel after dark, which was dangerous. In fact on a few occasions, she was molested, which involved unpleasant duties like filing FIRs. This encouraged Binalakshmi to become an activist with respect to women's rights and created confidence in her to deal with rough situations: for example, she could punch a molester on the nose before handing him over to the police, something that she could not have managed earlier.

After receiving her master's degree from the University of Delhi in 1997, Binalakshmi applied for admission to another highly respected centre of learning in Delhi: Jawahar Lal Nehru University (JNU), known as 'the Oxford of the East'. She gained admission in the M.Phil course in the School of International Studies. The university was known for its leftist leanings. Binalakshmi discovered great dedication amongst her politically inclined colleagues, and this influenced her own attitudes. She lived in the hostel on campus so she got easily absorbed into the JNU way of life, which she found very stimulating. She loved the academic atmosphere, particularly the post-dinner political discussions by moonlight in the gardens.

Meanwhile, her parents were concerned about her future and suggested that she appear for the government services examinations. They also dropped hints about getting married and starting a family. However, Binalakshmi reveled in her PhD at JNU. She worked very hard at her research. During the days, she studied in libraries as well as learnt from knowledgeable people through interviews. During the nights, she developed her research work. And during the late nights and early mornings, she buried herself in creative work—in her novel, *Meckley*. In the year 2000, when she was 26, she presented her dissertation on the subject 'Small Wars and Insurgencies in South Asia' to the School of International Studies at JNU—a magnificent achievement for a girl who started her studies in a little school in faraway Manipur.

At JNU, Binalakshmi systematically researched the armed conflict situation in Manipur and often travelled there to collect primary data. It was during one of these visits that she had become witness to the brutal killing of Budhi Moirangthem. She says: 'I realized then that there was no point in doing research if intervention did not follow. When you research on a topic two things may happen—you can research more, write more and become a philosopher or you can do something about the issue. I chose the second option, which was the path of action.' After completing her studies, she was determined to educate people about the grand past of Manipur, which had a civilization spanning two thousand years, and to work for the creation of a new society free from the menace of guns.

An international survey conducted by the United Nations showed that India had the most number of small arms in the hands of civilians. Small arms licenses were easily granted, and punishment for holding unlicensed arms was lenient. The easy availability of arms led to violence, and many young people took to the path of guns, leading todestruction—social, political and economic.

The UN had addressed the issue of small arms proliferation by launching its Programme of Action for Small Arms
and Light Weapons (UNPOA for SA & LW). This programme was not taken seriously by many countries, but in
India, it was seen as providing an opportunity to take
action against the gun culture. However, although India
submitted frequent reports to the UN on small arms issues,
there was no progress on the ground. Noting this,
Binalakshmi and her colleagues in the Manipur Gun
Survivors' Network decided to mobilize civil society to
address issues relating to the proliferation of small arms.

The Control Arms Foundation of India

In 2004, Binalakshmi cofounded India's first civil society
dedicated to disarmament—Control Arms Foundation of
India (CAFI) —and was its first secretary general. CAFI is
committed to stop the proliferation of small arms, which
had fueled violence in Manipur as well as in other northeastern states. It is a women-led movement that ensures
that divisive political, civil and social issues are dealt with
through informed debate, which creates public awareness, rather than through violence.

CAFI advocates controls in small arms trading so that
criminals cannot obtain guns. It also advocates safeguards
against illicit sale of weapons and their recycling as well
as the surveillance of stockpiles because such weapons
are vulnerable to diversion, pilferage and copying. CAFI
works through promoting research, advocacy, discussions
and awareness programmes to change attitudes. It also
engages with disarmament officials, parliamentarians,
think tanks and other NGOs on matters concerning armed

violence and weaponization. CAFI has produced three films on gun control issues: *Gun Wars and Drug Deaths, Gunning for Control* and *The Story of the Manipuri Women Gun Survivors*. It also organizes photo presentations, apart from seminars and conferences.

CAFI is also active in the sensitive area of the role of state-controlled armed forces. It encourages discussions and studies on the way these forces should operate. It supports the UN's Basic Principles on the Use of Force and Firearms by Law Enforcement Officials and organizes training of security forces in applying these principles. CAFI also works to strengthen the coordination between programmes of international organizations and development agencies so that they work in tandem. It strives to include small arms control and violence reduction into international, multinational and regional frameworks such as SAARC, BIMSTEC and so on.

The Northeast India Women Initiative for Peace

The Northeast India Women Initiative for Peace (NEIWIP) is another movement in which Binalakshmi played a leading role. It is a network of women's groups from all over the Northeast that are working for peace. The northeast region is home to many population groups speaking different languages and dialects. Vociferous and violent demands by different groups for independence and for new states have often resulted in continual militancy. No other region in India has seen such a proliferation of militant outfits as the Northeast.

In India's northeast region, women have traditionally played a major role in the economic sphere as is demonstrated by the many self-help groups, cooperatives, women's markets and so on However, women's perspectives and capabilities as peacemakers have remained underutilized, and their role in conflict resolution has been minimal, in spite of the United Nations Security Council passing a resolution to secure the involvement of women in conflict resolution and peacemaking as well as a UN convention for the elimination of discrimination against women. The NEIWIP seeks to remedy this situation. It helps women to get involved with issues like militancy and social reform by providing a platform for bringing together women from all walks of life, including academicians, lawyers, social activists and students, and giving them a voice. It encourages women from the northeastern states to work together for building peace and providing justice and political rights through participation in decision making as well as in policy formulation and in the implementation of processes that affect their lives.

The idea of creating the NEIWIP first came up in 2009 and then received a major fillip in 2012, when there was a sudden exodus of emotionally hurt northeast youngsters from cities such as Bengaluru, Pune, Mumbai and Delhi. These youngsters had been repeatedly told that people from the Northeast were outsiders; they were referred to as 'tribals' and called 'chinkis'. At that time, many questions about identity started cropping up. It was soon evident that such negative views about people from the Northeast needed to be addressed immediately.

Binalakshmi says: 'There are 45 million people in the Northeast and we are an integral part of India. Then why are we misunderstood and misrepresented? At NEIWIP, we realized that there was no point blaming the media. We then pointed out that the government agencies were not doing their job properly, and indeed they were not. People learn the most in the early years of their life and so we decided to approach the educational bodies of our country to ensure that the Northeast was properly presented in educational curricula and textbooks. In the past the Northeast had been poorly portrayed in Indian schoolbooks. (Often the only mention about the Northeast was that Cherrapunji in Assam had the highest rainfall!)'

The Future

The Manipur Gun Survivors' Network was severely handicapped in its task of supporting victims of militancy because the Manipur economy had been devastated by decades of civil war, which paralyzed economic activity. So the network was restricted in its efforts to provide livelihoods to widows. It was able to provide opportunities to start businesses only in a few traditional occupations. Of these traditional occupations, handicrafts had the best potential as many of the widowed gun survivors were already familiar with these items. However, the handicrafts sector in Manipur faced problems. For example, markets for these products were restricted to local areas and to local customers who had low demand and low capacity to pay. To enable Manipuri handicrafts to get a wider exposure and earn better returns for the war widows, certain issues needed to be urgently addressed: design inputs made available so that the products were adapted to modern tastes; quality upgraded by use of modern production techniques, equipment and materials; access to larger national and international markets enabled through showrooms in major markets and online platforms on the Internet for the convenience of customers who wished to buy merchandise without travelling to Manipur.

Dealing with such matters involves a new kind of expertise, of which Binalakshmi had no previous knowledge
or experience. For her, this work was of an altogether
different kind, making her future exciting but also challenging. She is going about this by putting in place a team
of professional people who have the required expertise
like designers, merchandisers and marketers who will
work in the artisanal units of the widows.

The future will also call upon Binalakshmi to devote
efforts to the problem concerning negative attitudes and
discrimination towards people from the Northeast. The
Government of India has already appointed her as a
member on its committee to look at issues concerning the
Northeast.

The issue of discrimination against people from the
Northeast again came into sharp focus recently in January
2014 when Nido Tania, an Arunachal boy, was beaten to
death in New Delhi's Lajpatnagar district. Also shocking
was the callous manner in which the episode was treated
by the public and by the local law-enforcing administration. Binalakshmi of course took a leading role in the
demonstrations to publicize the handling of this shameful
crime. Then in July 2014, a young man from Manipur,
Akha Salouni, was killed in an unprovoked discriminatory hate attack in South Delhi. Media reports continue to
indicate that discrimination against northeasterners is
not abating.

Binalakshmi's underlying thought on this subject of
discrimination is that once one knows a people, one feels
for them; this feeling had been missing with respect to
people from the Northeast, mainly because of lack of
knowledge. School and college education in India provides little awareness about people from the Northeast.

She says: 'The histories of millions of our citizens living in the northeastern states have been absent from our books. The consequent lack of awareness is one of the main reasons for discrimination against people from the Northeast.'

Incidentally, the Northeast has a lot of oral history in the form of folktales, ballads and lullabies, but this mine of information has not been studied and recorded systematically. Recently, with encouragement from Binalakshmi, a joint team of the Manipur Gun Survivors' Network and the NEIWIP together with the Indian Council of Historical Research has started documenting all available historical data and weaving the histories of the northeastern states into the mainstream of teaching in India.

All this indicates that the future for Binalakshmi promises to be full of opportunities to contribute to the uplifting of lives of the people of Manipur as well as of the Northeast and thereby of the country, which would be accomplished through her unique flair for combining action, dedicated perseverance and hard work.

9

Urvashi Butalia

Feminist Publishing

Urvashi Butalia is the pioneer of feminist publishing in India as well as a prominent activist and writer on women's issues. She belongs to a family of Sikh refugees from West Pakistan who left Lahore after partition and migrated to India to settle in Ambala, which was then in the Indian state of Punjab. Urvashi was born there in 1952. Her father was a journalist, and her mother was a teacher who, incidentally, had also been involved in supporting feminist issues such as the anti-dowry movement. In fact, to Urvashi, her mother served as an exemplar of women fighting for their rights.

Urvashi went to school and college in Delhi and graduated from Miranda House. Later, she obtained her master's degree in English literature from the University of Delhi and another Master's degree in South Asian Studies from the School of Oriental and African Studies in London. Her early work assignments were with the Oxford University Press (OUP) in New Delhi and later in Oxford as well as with Zed Books, a publishing company in London.

When Urvashi was at university in Delhi, it was a time of considerable political and social turbulence in India. She became deeply involved with student activist groups. It was in Miranda House, interacting with the bright and aware undergraduate girls there, that she became interested in women's issues, something that was to become a lifelong commitment.

Although she enjoyed the study of literature, Urvashi found it somewhat frustrating that courses at the University of Delhi in those days were still so caught within the colonial mould. Studying literature basically meant studying English literature—there were only very few optional papers that looked at other literature. This convinced her to not take up teaching, which would have been the predictable thing to do. She was keen to do something that was more connected to the ground realities of her life in India, rather than focus on the literature of another land.

This was also what led her to seriously consider publishing as a career. As she was keen to build up the stock of knowledge about women in India, Urvashi even dreamt of setting up a small printing press in her home, where she could print feminist texts and radical political pamphlets. This dream did not materialize, but neither did it entirely go away. It became the seed of an idea that would shape the rest of her life. Unexpectedly, she got some work, which involved publishing; this happened when a friend who worked with OUP suggested she do some freelance work there. Urvashi took up the suggestion and immensely enjoyed the work. It seemed to her that she had found her calling, which reconfirmed to her that publishing would be the appropriate career for her. As it happened, OUP offered Urvashi a job as an assistant to the production manager.

Urvashi also happens to be a leader who enjoys building organizations and working with people. She communicates easily with people from all levels of society. But leadership, she feels, does not come naturally. Like many other capabilities, it needs to be learnt and nurtured. According to Urvashi, it is her involvement in the feminist movement over the years that taught her a great deal about the importance of creating an egalitarian and inclusive work environment. Feminist collectives were her training ground for strategies that later became part of her management style. She learnt about giving a fair hearing to all points of view, the need to maintain calm and balance even in the face of contrarian viewpoints and the need to fairly give credit where it is due and to not appropriate all the credit to oneself. For her, a good leader is someone who works hard and is only as good as the team one builds. Urvashi is generous with her time, providing advice and support to women in need even if they are not professionally connected with her; she often goes further than expected by providing some additional help that a needy woman may require, such as paperwork to obtain various official permissions and registrations and even opening bank accounts and getting identity documents. It is mainly because of Urvashi's leadership style that her office generally is a happy place where everyone feels a sense of belonging and ownership.

While she was working at OUP, Urvashi also became more deeply involved in feminist activism. The anti-dowry and anti-rape campaigns had gathered considerable momentum at the time, and activists who were involved felt they needed to understand the roots of structural and systemic violence against women. Material on these issues was not easy to find, and indeed not much research had been done on them. Concerned at this, Urvashi says: 'I talked with my bosses at OUP, and said to them, why don't we do some books by women, about women? They did not seem to be at all interested. So then I thought, okay, if they won't do it, I'll do it myself. That was a hasty initial reaction; but then the idea started to take shape in my head and I began to work towards implementing it.'

It took a few years for the idea to take concrete shape. In 1978, Urvashi left the OUP to take up work at a college in the University of Delhi, teaching a professional course in publishing. By this time, she had decided to set up a feminist publishing house which, she hoped, would respond to the issues and questions being raised in the women's movement and would try to put together a body of knowledge by and about women that could help activists in the movement. Her hope was that such a publishing house would be economically independent and commercially viable. This was a tough call, because at that time, there was not much common reading interest in feminist issues, and this area was generally regarded with scepticism and considered to be a nonstarter.

Urvashi taught for a few years and then went to England where she worked for two years with Zed Books, helping set up their women's list of books by and about women from what was then called the Third World.

Launching Feminist Publishing

When Urvashi returned to India in 1984, she founded Kali for Women—India's first exclusively feminist publishing house, in partnership with Ritu Menon, a publisher with similar ideas and values. Urvashi and Ritu were driven by a passion to get women's voices heard. They wanted to help deepen the understanding of women's issues, provide material on the historical and cultural backgrounds of contemporary debates and to help connect with feminist movements internationally. They knew that initially, the reception for feminist books would perhaps not be very enthusiastic—the subject was new, the market yet to be created—so at Kali, they also took on editorial and publishing consultancies, which would allow them to raise some money that could be put towards publishing.

Urvashi and Ritu had contributed some initial funding to start Kali for Women. For a few of the early books, they sought grants from donor agencies and supplemented these with the money earned from their consultancies, paying themselves nothing. Within a few years, Kali was breaking even and was no longer dependent on donations—a commercial success story even by demanding banking standards!

Over two decades, Urvashi and Ritu, with the support of their dedicated teams, grew Kali to become a nationally and internationally recognized publishing house. It provided a forum for creative, academic, social and political writing by women and published pathbreaking works such as Radha Kumar's *The History of Doing* and Vandana Shiva's *Staying Alive* as well as *Recasting Women: Essays in Colonial History* by Kumkum Sangari and Sudesh Vaid.

Then there was a setback. After about two decades of working together and building Kali for Women, Urvashi and Ritu decided to part company. They felt that because of tension between them due to different styles of managing, a parting of ways would help the growth of feminist publishing. They shut down Kali for Women and instead founded two separate and independent publishing houses. Urvashi founded Zubaan, and Ritu founded Women Unlimited. Both publishing houses had an agenda similar to Kali for Women. Urvashi differentiated Zubaan by incorporating features such as general interest books, translations and children's books as well as books for differently abled readers and e-books. Zubaan also involved itself in arranging high-visibility projects in areas of feminist interest.

Years later, in 2011, both Urvashi and Ritu were honoured by the Government of India for their contribution to Indian publishing and awarded the Padma Shri.

The Major Challenge

The major challenge that the team at Zubaan faced when starting work was related to business economics. This resulted from the growing competition in the publishing industry. Kali for Women had become a known brand, so Zubaan already had a formidable benchmark standard to meet. The arrival of the two new feminist publishing houses raised concerns about whether there was enough space in the market for both. Moreover, at the turn of the century, there was a spurt in the number of publishers in India including several with British and American connections. Many of these publishers had noted the success of Kali for Women and therefore began to enter the feminist area, thus sharpening the competition. All this impacted the economics of small publishers like Zubaan, which had to match the high rates for inputs and services such as printing as well as the fees and salaries paid to writers, editors and other service providers. Most of these service providers preferred to work with the established mainstream publishers, and this was reflected in the fees they quoted to new young companies like Zubaan. Other challenges stemmed from the way the publishing industry in India is structured. It is based on a system that requires providing credits at various stages of the publication process, resulting in severe cash flow pressures, which make it very difficult for new small firms to enter and succeed.

Another big challenge for Zubaan, and indeed for other small independent publishers, was managing distribution. Without the bargaining power that comes with a large backlist and its attendant commercial 'clout', it was difficult to track payments as well as negotiate discounts. Ensuring that books—and authors—got the visibility in bookstores and in the media that they deserved, had always been a vital concern at Zubaan, especially as it was an important way to attract and retain new authors. However, Zubaan's small team did not have the personnel to handle multiple bookstore accounts.

While founding Zubaan, Urvashi had said: 'I want to see small feminist publishing houses survive and grow with their missions intact in a commercial market.' That statement of mission set the standards that Zubaan strived to achieve, as well as its organizational goals.

Related Activities

Apart from establishing Zubaan, Urvashi wrote (and continues to write) extensively on a broad spectrum of issues concerning women's rights and interests, from a modern and liberal viewpoint. For example, about the rights of live-ins, about transgenders, about unwed destitute mothers and about a host of issues concerning topics such as immolation of widows and rape. Her writing often used material from oral histories. She wrote several books and is the author of *The Other Side of Silence*, one of the most influential books written in the past decade concerning South Asia. It won the Oral History Book Association Award in 2001 as well as the Nikkei Asia Award for Culture in 2003. *The Other Side of Silence* has become a key work about the partition of India, which is still used in literary courses in Indian universities.

The partition of India caused one of the most massive human convulsions in history. In 1947, millions of people were displaced and many died within a span of a few months. Women were abducted and raped and children disappeared. Yet little was written about the human dimensions of this event. In *The Other Side of Silence*, Urvashi tried to fill this gap. The book was the outcome of over 70 interviews conducted over a 10-year period with survivors of the partition as well as studies of letters, diaries and memoirs from that period. It focuses particularly on how women, children and ordinary people were affected by this upheaval. It reflects on vital questions such as: What was the partition meant to achieve, and what did it actually achieve? What did community, caste and gender have to do with the violence that accompanied partition? How, in spite of unspeakable horrors, did the survivors carry on? Urvashi points out that the partition—like the holocaust—is very much 'living history', which still impacts current events.

To understand how and why certain events related to the partition became shrouded in silence, she looked at the experiences of her own and other partition-scarred family histories. This revealed that the voices of people affected by the partition had not been stilled and that bitterness remained. Urvashi wrote her book partly in the belief that only by remembering and telling their stories could those affected begin the process of healing and forgetting. The book is a sensitive and moving account of her quest to listen to the painful truth behind the silence.

Besides publishing, Urvashi and her team at Zubaan work on various projects related to women's issues. Many of these are in collaboration with well-known international development agencies. One of the projects they are currently working on is a South Asia-wide research project called *Sexual Violence and Impunity*, which involves commissioning a large number of research papers by individuals and groups in India, Pakistan, Bangladesh, Sri Lanka and Nepal. This project is funded by the Canadian International Development Research Centre. Another major project is 'Cultures of Peace', which showcases the diverse cultures of India's northeast through writing, music, film, theatre and media. The project is organized in collaboration with the Heinrich Böll Foundation. Zubaan has also worked with the Heinrich Böll Foundation on other issues, one of them being a series of lectures on the Partition entitled *Partition: The Long Shadow*, which have been gathered in a book by the same name. An earlier project, funded by the Ford Foundation, focused on mapping, through posters, a visual history of the women's movement. Through this project called 'Poster Women', Zubaan put together a unique collection of over 1,500 posters made by women's groups in different parts of India. The Poster Women archive is a fascinating pageant depicting the history of feminism in India and is now accessible online. It resulted in several major exhibitions, two books, postcards and associated merchandise. Zubaan also led a study that explored women's museums all over the world. This was in collaboration with the Ford Foundation.

However, publishing remains the core activity of Zubaan, and its team especially prefers to bring out books that are written by the new subaltern writers who often have no formal education or training. Often, such writers are from poor families living in slums who have had limited educational opportunities. Their stories are about life in those difficult circumstances and are very different from the works of the educated, English-speaking, city-dwelling, upper-middle-class women. The publication of the works of subaltern writers often brought about positive changes in the lives of the writers and of the readers, which was, in any case, a major objective of Zubaan's mission.

An example of this kind of subaltern publishing was the memoirs of a domestic worker named Baby Halder. Baby had a difficult life as a child; her mother left the family and went away with Baby's infant brother. Unable to deal with his children after his wife had gone, Baby's father first married off her elder sister and then Baby who was just a little over 12. Her husband was 14 years her senior. By the age of 13, Baby was a mother; she lived through a difficult and violent marriage, and finally one day, unable to take any more, walked out with her three children and came to Delhi. In Delhi, after much difficulty, and many false starts, she finally found a job in the house of a retired professor. Professor Prabodh Kumar was not only an academic but also the grandson of one of India's best-known Hindi story writers Munshi Premchand. The professor noticed that while cleaning his house, Baby paid a lot of attention to his books, and one day, he asked her if she could read. He then encouraged her to do so, lending her books and ensuring that she had time to read them. In this way, Baby taught herself once again to read. One day, the professor gave her a notebook and a pen and asked her to write about her life. The book she wrote, called *Alo Andhari* (From Darkness to Light), was published in English by Zubaan and became a trailblazer for many other similar books by marginalized women.

It was while working as a maid in Professor Kumar's home that Baby began serious writing. She wrote late at night, after work and sometimes in between chores such as sweeping, swabbing and mopping. The work was translated by Professor Kumar into Hindi and published. Urvashi came across the Hindi edition and immediately contacted the author and publishers for rights. She signed up, translated the book into English and published it under the title *A Life Less Ordinary*. The publication of this book transformed Baby Halder's life. She became an icon for other domestic workers. She gave talks about her life and her writings in many parts of the country as well as abroad. Later, she went on to write three more books. Each book took her a year to write as she chose to write while continuing to work as a domestic servant and looking after her children—she said this was necessary for her as it provided inspiration and material for her writing. Her books were translated into French, German and Japanese.

Within Zubaan, and earlier in Kali, Urvashi's team always made a special effort to support the voices of marginalized women. In 1989, Kali published a book called *Shareer ki Jankari* (About the Body). The book was written by 75 women from villages in Rajasthan. It was about female bodies. The women did not have the wherewithal to print it.

Urvashi says: 'When these women met us with the book, they imposed only one condition: that the book would not be sold for a profit. We started with a print run of 2,000, but before the copies had arrived from the printers, the women had canvassed in villages and presold 1,800 copies. Over the years, some 70,000 copies have been sold!'

Another book that is important to Zubaan is *Do You Remember Kunan Poshpora*, written by a group of five young Kashmiri women, all in their 20s; it explores the history of a case of mass rape in 1991 in two villages in Kashmir, Kunan and Poshpora. Keen to explore their history, and to reopen this case, the women wanted to write a book. They contacted Zubaan not only to ask the publisher whether it would be interested in the book but also with an unusual request: They said that although they had all the material, they did not really know how to put it together as a book and wanted Zubaan to teach them. Zubaan then invited them to Delhi and conducted a two-day writing workshop in which the young women were taught the technicalities of case writing by the Zubaan team. They then went back to Kashmir and produced a full-length manuscript, which is soon to be published as a book by Zubaan.

This is the kind of publishing that was always very important for Urvashi because it represented a lot of what she considered to be vital in her own mission in life. It also motivated Urvashi's team of like-minded associates.

Urvashi has also been very active in Indian and global women's movements. She has worked with groups who have been engaged in bringing about change in laws on violence against women, dowry and rape. She is now working on a new book named *Mona: A Sort of Life/A Life of Sorts*, which is about the life of a eunuch.

Urvashi's Advice to Aspiring Entrepreneurs

Too often, girls in India are told what will be good for them instead of encouraging them to apply their own minds. But it is important for young girls to be able to dream, to look at what they really want to do, to believe in themselves and to let their imaginations roam free. A strong belief in what you want to do is the first step towards achieving it. And if you do succeed in setting up something, bear in mind that the enterprise is more important than you and that it deserves to continue even after you.

The Future

The success of the Zubaan team in terms of the quality and variety of its publications and their impact as well as the success of its projects and its overall standing in the industry has given Urvashi the confidence to think of scaling up its activities considerably. The expansion programme that the Zubaan team has been considering also involves a diversification of activities; for example, to overcome the financial problems arising from being a small publishing house, Zubaan would now also enter new areas of work such as providing consultancy services related to publishing and thus get better cash flows. It would provide services that several organizations desperately need, such as advising organizations about issues like gender sensitization, prevention of sexual harassment at work and so forth. Providing such services would also allow the optimal use of the wide professional network that Zubaan has developed over the years.

A key issue here is that the programme of expansion and diversification would require substantial external funding. Zubaan was originally set up as a not-for-profit trust. Alongside this trust, Zubaan recently established a for-profit commercial company called Zubaan Publishers Pvt. Ltd, which is owned by senior Zubaan staff. This for-profit company, unlike the trust, will be eligible to seek and obtain external commercial investments that could be used to finance its growth programme.

Zubaan is now seeking a partner (or partners) that could provide the investment to fund its future growth. Ideally, it is looking for a partner whose philosophy is in sync with its own and which is in harmony with its existing management style and structure. Given the kind of business that publishing is, and the kind of organization that Zubaan in particular is, it would need to be an investor that is primarily more interested in social impact, particularly in impacting the lives of women rather than its own financial gain.

Zubaan is on the threshold of becoming a unique and powerful hub to promote women's interests while being organizationally sound and economically viable. It is vital at this stage that Urvashi manages to secure the cooperation of an appropriate partner that will support its work.

10
Manisha Gupta

Social Entrepreneurship

Manisha Gupta, an intrepid and inspiring woman entrepreneur, is the founder and managing director of StartUp, an organization devoted to helping budding social entrepreneurs incubate their projects. It provides development and execution support to seed and scale up ventures that create lasting social change, particularly in marginalized sections of society. Manisha explains the thinking behind her venture: 'StartUp is a social development enterprise. We work in a deeply embedded partnership with social entrepreneurs from an early stage to the stage when their enterprise is self-sufficient. We provide the management support that an enterprise needs to become process and systems driven, to become resilient and to have a strategic orientation, so that it can scale up without too many trials and errors as well as avoid expensive mistakes. In this way, we almost become limited co-partners in the enterprise.'

Ideas concerning her future mission in life started taking shape in Manisha's mind at an early age. While she was still a little girl in school in Kolkata, she noticed unfair happenings around her, particularly concerning the treatment of girls. She says: 'I grew up in a large family and I saw how girls were restricted in many ways, while boys had greater mobility. Generally girls were treated as inferior to boys and were given fewer facilities. This favouritism was so rampant that both boys and girls accepted it as normal and natural. I also noticed other happenings in our society which conflicted with my ideas of just conduct; these included our discriminatory treatment of people from other castes, other communities and other religions and sometimes even extended to people with a different colour of skin! Noticing these practices made me wonder how conditions could be improved.'

Years later as an undergraduate student of humanities at St Xavier's College from 1991 to 1994, she acquired the conceptual background and the vocabulary to formulate her thoughts into a coherent goal and mission.

During her student days, Manisha also started writing as a freelance journalist for newspapers and magazines.

This writing considerably helped her sort out her ideas and develop the ability to express herself.

Background

Manisha's family comes from the Gupta clan, a part of a trading fraternity that migrated from Varanasi to Kolkata around the turn of the century and established a very successful Indian sweetmeat business. The sweetmeat business in Kolkata did very well and soon expanded to include establishments in Bahrain, Kathmandu and even London. The success of the business enabled the family to develop connections with influential people including, for example, the Birla family who were then considered the doyens of Marwari business in Kolkata. These contacts resulted in spin-offs, which further benefitted the Gupta business. Manisha grew up in this environment where entrepreneurial business ideas were continually discussed and debated; so she had the entrepreneurial instinct in her genes, and from early childhood, she was exposed to a business culture and atmosphere.

The Gupta family was deeply traditional and old-fashioned in their outlook and beliefs. It was strongly patriarchal, and orders from the senior menfolk were meant to be obeyed without question or argument. Elders presided over all family matters, including decisions regarding the education, marriage and career choices of its members, in a regimented, control-and-command manner. There was tremendous pressure to follow the path that had been laid down by the family elders. If one tried to break away from the approved way, one would not be tolerated. Growing up in such a conservative family strangely served to strengthen, rather than weaken, Manisha's desire to step out and create an individual identity of her own.

Manisha's father was somewhat different from the rest of the family. He had travelled widely to work on his dream of setting up a chain of world-class Indian confectionary stores in foreign countries. He was fairly liberal in his views and a bit of an iconoclast. He opened new windows that encouraged liberal views and brought fresh energy into the family. He introduced young Manisha to theatre, dance and books and also shielded her from some of the archaic traditional family pressures. But unfortunately, this shield was not to last for very long.

Manisha's comfortable existence was shattered, and she suffered a big shock when suddenly one day her father died in a road accident at the age of 33. Manisha was then 11 years old and was already developing a mind of her own. Apart from the grief of losing a parent, Manisha also suffered the loss of protection provided by his liberal views in a traditional environment.

Another event that greatly affected Manisha occurred at about this same time: The girls school that she had been attending, and which was commonly regarded as Kolkata's archetypical academy for traditional values and hence accepted as 'safe' by her family, soon acquired a new principal, a Ms Shobhana Verghese, who immediately started changing the culture of the school. For example, instead of teaching the girls embroidery and the domestic pastimes of a typical Hindu bahu, the school began to emphasize teaching some of the up-to-date modern skills such as public speaking, theatre, shorthand, typing and so forth. This change of emphasis at school struck a sympathetic chord with Manisha who was further encouraged to confront and deny old-fashioned beliefs about the role of women in society.

The conflict between the traditional and the modern came up repeatedly throughout Manisha's childhood and youth, particularly when matters concerning her work and her lifestyle were under consideration. The conflict took centre stage when the contentious question about Manisha's marriage came up. Her grandparents announced that a suitable boy had been found in Agra and that he would shortly be visiting 'to look at the girl'. Manisha forcefully put her foot down on any expectations about an arranged marriage and asked the family to desist from finding suitors for her. The family's reaction to Manisha's stand was immediate and severe. She was locked up in her room and all doors to the outside world were slammed shut. She also experienced physical violence. The clan had never before encountered a family girl saying no to a marriage proposal introduced by the family and then seeking a different life involving higher education and career. They were enraged, to put it mildly.

At this time, some of the family's influential friends including teachers from the Birla-controlled girls school intervened and persuaded Manisha's grandfather to agree to letting her step out of the house and work at least within the boundaries of a nine-to-five time line. About that distressing time, Manisha made a significant statement: 'After experiencing that confinement, when I did step out, I made a profound personal resolution. It was that no circumstance, no individual, nobody would henceforth determine my decisions and my movements. I would build my own life and take responsibility for it.'

This was a life-altering resolve that put Manisha firmly on the path of social change, particularly on working with issues concerning women's rights.

After the distressing showdowns with her family, for the first time in her young life, Manisha felt challenged and struggled to cope with life's problems. At this time, just as StartUp was being established, she derived solace and strength from a growing belief in Nichiren Daishonin Buddhism. She took up this study seriously and participated in related events including community prayers and chanting—a form of dynamic meditation and the bedrock of this Buddhist practice—and it enabled her to empower herself to build her life force, lift her energy levels and strengthen her spiritual life. From this practice, she understood that one's external environment was a reflection of one's inner being. So if she did not like something or someone, she needed to change her attitude and perception, and the problem would get resolved.

These Buddhist practices developed an inner strength in Manisha. She gradually began to assert her independence. She again began to write as a freelance journalist. Knowing her family's aversion to journalism particularly as work for females, Manisha was careful to hide her identity by omitting bylines and focussing on publications that she knew her family would not read.

By the time she left university, Manisha had decided to commit her life to bringing about social change in Indian society, particularly for women and for the underprivileged sections of society. She then began searching for institutions that could help her achieve her objective. She recounts, 'As a young person with many questions about issues of equity and inclusion, I searched for organizations that could help me achieve my mission. A chance encounter led me to the doorstep of Ashoka: Innovators for the Public—a global organization working to promote social entrepreneurship. This was in 1994. I had not then understood the term social entrepreneur. I did not understand what it meant. But I sensed a tremendous possibility and energy.'

The Ashoka India office at that time was tucked away in a small corner of a large warehouse in central Kolkata. There, in an office that could barely seat more than four people, Manisha met Sushmita Ghosh, then the country representative for India, who later went on to become the Global President of Ashoka. 'Sushmita spoke of concepts that were way, way out of my radar. But her understated brilliance and grasp of concepts of social entrepreneurship were so powerful that I could not turn away', Manisha recalls. Manisha was impressed by Ashoka: Innovators for the Public and particularly its chief Ms Sushmita Ghosh.

Manisha joined Ashoka after graduating in 1994. She worked there for nine years in various positions including India country representative as well as the international director for Ashoka's young social entrepreneur programmes. She developed new initiatives to build a collaborative community of social entrepreneurs in the country and launched Ashoka's marketing, communication and brand building programmes in India. She edited Ashoka India's house magazine *The Changemakers*, which later transitioned to the Internet as www.changemakers.net.

It was while working at Ashoka that Manisha noticed the various ways in which a woman entrepreneur committed to social change could make a positive difference to Indian society, and by the time she was nearing the end of her assignment at Ashoka, the idea of establishing StartUp had begun to take root in her mind. But she knew then that she did not have the necessary experience and skills to get StartUp going. For example, she lacked experience of working inside a grassroots-level field-based hands-on social welfare enterprise. So after working for 10 years as a senior executive at Ashoka, Manisha decided to go back to working as an apprentice to gather experience relevant to her goals. She interned with four different social welfare enterprises to gain varied experience.

Equipped with her deeper understanding of how social welfare enterprises function, Manisha launched StartUp in 2007. After a two-year test-run, she set up the enterprise, formally, in 2009. The initial years were a struggle, but Manisha stayed committed to the larger mission of social change that her venture had set out to create. She believed that there was a demand from social ventures for incubatory services that would make them robust, process-focused and enable them to stand on their own feet. Support from organizations like StartUp would enable them to become attractive to investors and to talent.

Incidentally, it was also during this time when she was working with Ashoka that Manisha found the man she wanted to marry—Shubho Sengupta, an upcoming and bright digital media consultant from a liberal Bengali family. The announcement of her marital plan set off a major showdown in the family home. She was summoned by her grandparents and scolded for daring to take such a decision without consulting elders. She was told that if she married Shubho, she would be ostracized and would have to fend for herself. The family would not support or recognize her.

Manisha realized that she would have to take a tough stand to maintain her dignity and self-respect and the freedom to think out and make her destiny. She married Shubho and left the family home.

When she walked out of her family home, she entered the new ambience of a progressive family of Bengali intellectuals—her in-laws. Her husband's family became the wind beneath her wings and gave her the freedom and respect to chart her own course.

StartUp's Projects

StartUp was conceived as an angel investor, incubator and consultant to social entrepreneurs. As an investor, StartUp arranged financing from partner organizations as well as invested its time and expertise to establish and scale up social ventures. As an incubator, StartUp provided supportive services to practical business models that balance social impact with financial sustainability. As a consultant, StartUp worked with mature social ventures to accelerate their growth and impact so that their capabilities to promote social welfare activities were strengthened. In sum, StartUp helped launch, strengthen and scale up ventures that led to social development, particularly in marginalized communities and especially concerning women.

StartUp's work has been conducted in various fields and in various ways generally involving collaborative arrangements with other organizations including clients, incubatees, investors, well-wishers and like-minded bodies. Some examples of the outcomes of these arrangements show the breadth and sweep of StartUp's work:

- It supported training women from poor urban communities to become chauffeurs. These women were provided employment in a woman's cab and 'chauffeurs-on-call' service, which offered safe and reliable transport solutions to working women in Delhi.
- It supported an organization in southern Rajasthan that cared for seasonal migrant labourers through schemes that provided credit, promoted savings, got social security and promoted micro-investment projects.

- It co-founded Anveshaa with four leading social entrepreneurs. It is a professional association of grassroots-level women entrepreneurs, which enables members to communicate with policy makers, business associations and financial institutions. It centre-stages women entrepreneurs in India's growth story.
- In collaboration with the Swayam Shikshan Prayog, it co-created a 'centre for excellence' for rural women business leaders. It provided training, trade facilitation, marketing linkages, research and seed funding, particularly for green and clean projects.
- It supports the All India Artisans and Craft Workers Welfare Association—a trainer, advocate and ecosystem builder. Its Craftmark certification programme provides much-needed support through giving validation to craft-based small- and medium-sized enterprises (SMEs).
- In collaboration with the National Skill Development Corporation, it helps producer groups with disabilities through ARUNIM, which offers enterprise development exposure, product design, a common brand and access to finance and markets.
- It assists Amrit Clinics, a network of affordable primary healthcare clinics, for seasonal migrant labourers. It serves the most excluded, informal workforce of the country.
- It associates with Bombay Connect, which is a collaborative workspace for individuals who have the ideas and the passion for making good things happen. It offers an energized and well-connected work environment and networking opportunities for growth.

- It helps the Corporate Social Responsibility wing of JCB, a leading heavy-engineering company, to launch fellowships for high-school students in Haryana. This helps youngsters to transform their lives and become role models in their communities.
- It runs a short-term fellowship programme for students and young professionals who wish to work with Indian social entrepreneurs. It has hosted fellows from leading American and European academic institutions.
- It conducted a process evaluation of the Kasturba Gandhi Balika Vidyalayas across Uttar Pradesh. About this intervention, the client said: 'They developed a sound understanding of our programme and devised a long-term strategy. The team is thorough and goes the extra mile to ensure quality and value addition.'
- It served as the implementing partner for the Social Entrepreneur of the Year Award on behalf of the Jubilant Bhartia Foundation and Schwab Foundation for Social Entrepreneurship.
- It conducted impact assessments, monitoring and evaluation for international organizations such as the Ford Foundation's International Fellowships Program, PRADAN, International Centre for Research on Women and the Cherie Blair Foundation.
- It anchored the development of the country's first child protection standards in collaboration with the Childline India Foundation.

Amongst all these initiatives, Manisha considers the first initiative to be the most significant, which involved training women from poor families to become chauffeurs,

aptly called Women on Wheels. The Women on Wheels programme enables women from the poorer sections of urban
communities to become professional drivers and gain
remunerative employment. The programme also enhances
their awareness about women's rights and enables them to
become independent and confident individuals who are
able to make informed choices and decisions in life.

This project that well demonstrates StartUp's mission
and values is described in depth in the following section.

WOMEN ON WHEELS

In this project, StartUp teamed up with the Azad
Foundation, an NGO that trains women from resource-
poor urban communities to become professional and
commercial chauffeurs. These trained women drivers
are then provided employment through its strategic partner Sakha, a social business enterprise that offers safe
and reliable transport solutions to urban women. It
places professional women chauffeurs in families, in corporate houses and in the not-for-profit sector. It also runs
a women's cab business and a chauffeur-on-call service.
Sakha's programmes are designed to be managed by
women for women and provide decent livelihoods with
respect and dignity, which includes perquisites like provident fund, overtime, and paid leave. Together, StartUp,
the Azad Foundation and Sakha literally put 'women on
wheels'.

On this project, Manisha worked closely with Meenu
Vadera, Director of Azad, whose ideas and values are similar to those of Manisha. StartUp was first involved in con-
ceiving the 'big picture' of the Women on Wheels project.

Manisha and her team studied the urban transport industry in considerable depth. This involved interactions with the industry leaders and key players in the urban transport ecosystem. They conducted a thorough demand assessment through researching the market potential of major customer segments such as IT, BPO, Media and Healthcare. They also involved themselves in identifying and recruiting the key team leaders and functional experts. Apart from this hands-on support, StartUp worked on drawing up the strategic and operational plans of Azad and Sakha as well as their financial models and organizational structures. Together, Manisha and Meenu Vadera developed funding proposals and made joint pitches to investors.

The Women on Wheels programme started in 2008 in Delhi. Since then it has grown and is now also present in Gurgaon, Jaipur and Kolkata.

The impact of the Women on Wheels programme needs to be understood *not only in numbers but more importantly in the depth of the change* it brings to the trained women and their families and communities.

The transformation and empowerment that the Women on Wheels trainees achieve is irreversible. The programme enables women to identify the power within themselves, and once they connect with it, there is no going back. Furthermore, the benefits of the programme reach out to their children—girl children particularly, making an inter-generational impact of far-reaching consequences.

A majority of the women who complete the programme become the principal breadwinners in their families. They are not only financially independent but also capable of making their own decisions. Many trainees decide to continue with their studies and are also able to support the education of their children and of other family members. Others take on the responsibility of looking after the health issues of their parents or other family members by taking them for treatment, liaising with doctors and ensuring care. Some trainees are enabled to invest in a property in their own name and thus secure their future.

The women who undertake the programme and those already working as commercial drivers inspire other women to also take on nontraditional professions and become autonomous and economically independent.

To graphically illustrate the impact of the Women on Wheels programme in a manner that highlights the human angle, we provide below extracts from the stories of three among the several girls who benefitted from the programme. They are Shanti, Rajkumari and Chandni.

Shanti

Today, Shanti is a commercial chauffeur with Sakha. Quiet and confident, she inspires trust in her clients and is a role model for her three daughters who she is bringing up as a single mother. Shanti's husband walked out on her and her daughters a few years ago. Shanti was relieved when this happened as it was better to be without a husband than to be with one who was violent. Shanti and her daughters had suffered from the unpredictable bouts of his rage, almost on a daily basis, for many years.

When her husband left Shanti, she had studied only up to Class 10; she then desperately tried to look for a job—any job—that would help her sustain herself and her family. However, the jobs she was able to find were erratic, without guarantees, without leave and with very low salary and required putting in long hours of work, making it very difficult for Shanti to manage.

Shanti joined Azad to learn about driving, but she found a space where she could also learn much more. Through the gender classes especially, she found an opportunity to reflect on her own experiences and realized that she had different choices in life. Through the counselling sessions, she was able to understand how to deal with her personal challenges.

Eventually, with her own hard work and support from Azad, she gained professional competence and then took up employment as a chauffeur. She was employed by a visually impaired woman and worked with her for more than a year before joining Sakha as a commercial driver.

RAJKUMARI

Rajkumari is a 22-year-old woman from Jahangirpuri in North Delhi. Rajkumari's career dream was to be a police officer, but she had to leave her studies after the Class 8 because of economic difficulties in her family. Her elder sister was married off when she was 14 years old and went through a violent married relationship that also affected Rajkumari. Because of the difficult financial situation at home, Rajkumari took up a job of a maidservant along with her sister who by then had walked out of her violent marriage.

During the outreach and mobilization programme in Jahangirpuri, Rajkumari's sister picked up an Azad pamphlet and gave it to Rajkumari. Both sisters eventually enrolled in the programme. Rajkumari was initially shy and reserved but slowly started opening up and speaking about herself, her dreams and her fears. She now says that she would never tolerate violence in any way. Rajkumari cleared the Sakha test in May this year and is now getting ready to take up employment with a woman with special needs.

CHANDNI

At the age of four, Chandni along with her parents had migrated from their village to New Delhi. Chandni studied up to Class 10. She now lives in the Navjeevan camp in Govindpuri. In the women's community centre, she learnt embroidery and sewing. She heard about Azad there and also witnessed its street play. It was then that she realized that it was possible to do something new and different. Very soon thereafter, she registered at the Azad Foundation.

The course was rigorous but exciting. Going to Maruti's Institute of Driving Training and Research at Sarai Kale Khan was a matter of pride. The girls received hands-on experience on different cars, used simulators, and were given practical training on the roads as well. They were trained in self-defence by the Delhi Police, and they improved their interpersonal skills by attending communication classes. They were also exposed to many other socially relevant subjects such as women's rights and empowerment as well as sexual and reproductive health.

Chandni says: 'I now have courage and confidence in myself. I remember how timid I was before I joined Azad. Earlier, I was scared even to get into a bus, but now my day begins at 6.30 am and I return home by 10.30 pm. I love to drive and be independent. To earn on my own is now my passion. I have been working now for almost a year, and I earn ₹4,500 every month. If I work extra hours above my agreed time, I earn overtime, and sometimes when it gets late, my employers give me money to go home in a cab. I am thrilled to be earning so much. I have started a recurring deposit and have also appeared for my class 12 exams this year. I am now confident that wherever I am, even under the most stressful circumstances, I can sail through!'

'The best part of being a trained driver is being seen as being equal to a man. Driving is seen as a man's job and women are not trusted to do it. It is a brave thing for a girl to do. We change tyres in the middle of the road, like men do, and we don't care who is looking at us.'

—Saroj, a Sakha driver

Manisha: Personal Details

APPEARANCE

Manisha is one of those fortunate women whose age perpetually remains difficult to guess. Her lively temperament, agile movements and petite figure make her look perpetually youthful. She has short bobbed hair framing an expressive childish face generally with an earnest expression that easily breaks into a quick smile and then into laughter.

EXPERIENCE

Manisha has 20 years of experience in the social entrepreneurship sector in India. She has served as an advisor to several social entrepreneurs and their organizations and consulted with international funding agencies. Her areas of specialization are:

- Incubating and scaling high-impact social ventures in the domain of livelihoods, health as well as education;
- Strategy, financial modelling and business plan development;
- Hands-on, field-based, coaching on execution systems and processes;

- Knowledge creation, impact assessments and documentation of models and practices.

PUBLICATIONS

Since 2005, Manisha has been engaged in several country-wide research and impact assessment projects for various Indian and international social change organizations and documented the blueprints of their models.

- *Helpline 1098:* 10 Years of CHILDLINE in India, The Childline India Foundation, 2006–2007. (The book documents the blueprint of the Childline model and its strategies while culling out the good practices of advocating to and working with the government.)
- *The caste divide:* The Politics of Dalit disempowerment, 10 Years of grants to Organizations addressing Dalit reform in New Delhi, India, 2008—An assessment of The Ford Foundation, India's grant-making strategies to Dalit rights groups and a landscape assessment of the Dalit rights sector in India.
- *Opening doors:* Building social justice leadership and equity, 10 years of The Ford Foundations International Fellowship Program in India, 2012. (The study traces the journeys and impact of professionals trained to work with the poorest communities of India. It particularly notes the principles, strategies and challenges of engaging the youth of India to understand poverty.)
- *Women entrepreneurs in India and information communications technology (ICT):* Keys to an economic future, International Centre for Research on Women, 2011–2012—a research work focusing on

how information communication technology can promote SME women entrepreneurs in India.

Challenges Faced in Establishing StartUp

Manisha, in her own words, describes some of the major challenges she faced in the course of building StartUp:

Living with a bank account with zero balance: I had little savings to dip into, when I decided to work full-time in StartUp! Prior to this, I had worked in the not-for-profit sector for almost 15 years and had always brought home a salary, which was modest but enough for my needs. The first casualty after my decision to go full-time with StartUp was my personal finance and the esteem that was linked to my being financially independent. More than the loss of regular income, I had to deal with the idea of being financially dependent on my husband. This was very hard because I had been working and earning from the age of 18! Of course my husband was generous, but I was adamant about funding all my personal expenses—such as telephone bills, Internet bills and pur-chases of books (most important). So I drew on my small kitty of savings, and before I knew it, I had no balance in my bank account.

For more than a year, my personal bank balance hov-ered between ₹2,500 and ₹5,000. I grit my teeth through the period of zero income and reminded myself everyday of my larger mission of change and of the larger long-term non-material accruals that would come from being part of the country's social entrepreneurship sector. I struggled to stay hopeful everyday. My monetary situation became better after a year, and I started paying myself a salary of ₹15,000. The value of that ₹15,000 was incomparable. This period trained me to respect money and resources in ways that had a powerful impact.

Now when I look back, I realize that one cannot survive the perils of entrepreneurship unless (a) one is committed to a long-term mission and (b) one is aligned with a mission that is larger than making money.

Dealing with a partnership split: After two years of testing the incubation methodology of StartUp, I brought on board two partners who were designated as cofounders. One was based in Mumbai, and the other was based in Bengaluru. Both were from the corporate sector and had been part of the growth cycle of a large, international consulting firm. They brought a lot of technical and managerial skills to StartUp.

After a satisfactory period of setting the foundation and getting the basics right, as well as building the cofounder chemistry, the partnership split in two years. Both partners exited StartUp! It felt a bit like a tsunami at that time—it was brutal and sudden and came without warning. The partners recommended that we shut down StartUp! But that was unthinkable for me. I had not set myself on the path of entrepreneurship to close down the venture. StartUp was two years old then and had a mind and rhythm of its own. We could not put it to bed. So I decided to move forward and take the responsibility of rebuilding StartUp It took about a year to put matters to a close. This experience taught me a few critical lessons. These were:

- You may bring on board your best friends and closest relatives as business partners. But make sure you hire a lawyer and develop clear contracts with exit clauses for all partners. Make this a priority.

- Get the roles, accountabilities and governance right between all partners. Ensure that partners have clear revenue targets and their financial rewards are linked to the business they bring.
- Ask yourself—am I bringing partners on board because I want passionate entrepreneurs to co-create the journey with me? Or am I bringing on board skilled professionals who I will call cofounders simply because I don't have money to pay them now? The second option is a recipe for disaster.
- Take time and have multiple discussions with potential partners to identify those who are aligned to your mission. Ensure that in the early stages all partners are working out of the same city and from the same office. It is crucial to have face time. Proximity goes a long way in building a common mission.

Learning that work–life balance is a myth: My daughter Aanya was born in 2004 was five years old when I started building StartUp! I quickly learnt that the concept of work–life balance was never going to play itself out in a neat way in my life. And I was happy and relieved when that realization dawned on me. Once I let go of the expectation from my own self to maintain work–life balance, I became less stressed, less anxious and less edgy. I started to enjoy bringing up my daughter and building up StartUp in a seamless manner. I have found passion in both my roles—as a mother and as an entrepreneur, and therefore, questions of work-life balance don't bother me because being a mother and an entrepreneur are the core of my life, and life in itself is never balanced.

Like most women entrepreneurs who are responsible for looking after a family in addition to building their entrepreneurial venture, Manisha often felt torn between conflicting calls on her time. She says: 'I felt it is a duty to promote the wellbeing of my daughter, my husband, my mother and my in-laws. Fortunately for me, my family is supportive and I do not have to bear any strain on that count. My husband is quite content to not get involved in my work. He cheerfully adopted the role of acting as the banker for my financial needs and of providing emotional support if required. In fact, Manisha did not want Shubho to get too involved in StartUp's affairs—her policy was to maintain a strict distinction between her family and her work. When she was at home, she wanted to enjoy her family life and not carry any work worries home.

My daughter studies in a modern progressive school in Noida. She is doing well in her studies and school activities. She is a strong-willed and independent-minded girl—not dependant on getting attention from me. Manisha's work involves frequent travel often to remote places (which she loves!), but when she has to start packing, she does feel pain in leaving Aanya and also a feeling of guilt.'

Manisha's mother-in-law is a liberal Bengali intellectual. She is an astrophysician and lives in Kolkata. She visits Manisha in Delhi occasionally. Her father-in- law is no more. So Manisha manages to perform her family duties without creating too much stress and without distracting herself from her work.

Still, Manisha has decided not to have a second child. She says: 'I am a hands-on mom and a full-time entrepreneur. And this means that I have to do the work of two people, and keep time aside for myself. In juggling multiple matters, I have learnt that even as I focus on the sustainability of my business, I must also focus on the sustainability of my person, and continuously build my reserves of energy, resilience and life-force.'

With regard to challenges faced by women on account of gender, Manisha says that she is aware that women find it difficult to raise funds, hire talent and build supply/marketing chains for their start-ups. These challenges arise mainly because of apprehensions that a woman entrepreneur may abandon her venture for family reasons. This poses a serious problem. However, Manisha had become well aware of the nature of these problems during the nine years she had worked at Ashoka and uses that knowledge and experience to sidestep these problems. For example, she avoids going to markets to raise funds, to hire people, or to build business connections. She prefers to use internally generated funds or money collected from personal contacts and she finds and recruits personnel herself using informal channels.

The Future

Manisha sees the future of StartUp as providing support particularly to young social entrepreneurs from disadvantaged communities to expand their networks. This would involve setting up more incubators which would in turn create a new generation of capable and empathetic business coaches and mentors. Manisha will act according to her belief that the key to success is conviction in one's mission, nonstop hard work and resilience as well as surrounding oneself with supportive mentors, advisors and other entrepreneurs.

Manisha reflects: 'In my journey of discovery and growing up I started engaging with organizations that were working on issues of women's rights. Now with StartUp I seem to have come full circle in my quest to work for a more equitable society. For me the dots have begun to connect because when I look back, the bulk of work we have done is either with women social entrepreneurs, addressing women's rights or social entrepreneurs who are focused on ensuring that women from the most under-served communities are included in India's story. It has been very rewarding for me.

Many years ago, when I began my work with StartUp, many well-meaning advisors told me to, "harvest the low hanging fruit." But the seed had just been sown, there was no tree in sight and I could barely envision the shape, color and taste of any fruit. Over the years, and in good season, we have reaped a bumper crop of fruit— all of which have hung low; we have had to prepare hard and wait long for those seasons to arrive, and then the harvest has brought its own wisdom—that the fruit was never ours to claim, in the first place!'

Epilogue

The 10 entrepreneurial women featured in this book are involved in a variety of activities. They are of different age groups, education, family background and social status. Yet their inspiring stories show some commonality in the ways that they overcame prejudices and sociocultural challenges to establish their ventures.

Remarkably, none of these women entrepreneurs said that being female was a hindrance to starting their ventures. In fact, many mentioned the advantages of being a woman and some even joked about the outdated attitudes of males who did not appreciate the idea of women starting ventures.

To give back to society was a concern of many of these women entrepreneurs. In fact, often the projects selected by these women were such that they incorporated features that were aimed at benefitting the society. The implementation of the projects contributed to welfare, particularly of deprived sections of the society.

All the women demonstrated courage and an ability to take risks. Many of them put their entire life's savings into the start-up. However, these risks, though daring, were carefully calculated and taken after diligent research.

A popular notion prevails that in India, families discourage girls from starting ventures rather than attending to home affairs. This notion is not supported by the experiences narrated in the book, which indicate that the families gave moral support to the girls going out to start creative undertakings: Parents advised their daughters to fulfil their dreams, husbands were graciously accommodating with respect to their wives' hectic schedules and in-laws were supportive and helped in various ways such as minding the children when the mother was away. Interestingly, with respect to marriage, quite a few of the women entrepreneurs married late or did not marry at all, and this is a fact that deserves reflection.

The ability to work hard, often for long hours, with total commitment to the project is another significant characteristic that came up repeatedly in the experiences of these entrepreneurs. They were all deeply passionate about what they were doing. This did not mean that they toiled in dull work and drudgery. In fact, they all enjoyed their work. Had they not enjoyed their work, it is likely that they would not have been able to put in the effort required for success.

Continual learning appeared repeatedly in the work habits of these women, and this was demonstrated by a lack of hesitation to ask for help and guidance from professional experts, coaches and mentors as well as by visiting seminars, lectures and training courses where they could pick up useful relevant information. They were avid readers of professional books and journals related to their area of work. In addition, they networked with leaders in their fields to learn better ways of doing things. They treated learning and education as a continuing process.

These women who started the ventures were very clear about what they wanted to achieve in life. This is noteworthy, because in India, girls are often told what would be good for them instead of being encouraged to figure this out for themselves. This results in difficulty in formulating clear objectives.

Often entrepreneurs forget to consider how their venture will fare when they leave. Therefore, many good projects wither away after the founder exits. Entrepreneurs with foresight know that a time will come when they can no longer remain with the project, and they therefore plan in the beginning to make arrangements so that their venture will still survive and grow after them.

Many of these women paid serious attention to promptings from their inner voice and to their gut feelings. They also considered advice from well-wishers but took their own decisions finally after much rational thought.

The women entrepreneurs used different criteria for measuring the success of their undertakings. Interestingly, most of them did not consider size or profitability to be vital criteria. Factors that they considered significant included the contribution of their project to uplift society as well as its impact on the environment. Faithfully following the originally stated mission of the venture was also considered important.

The ability to scan the emerging socioeconomic scenario to discover opportunities helped these women identify areas where they could make an impact. Many of them used research to find demand–supply gaps. Before entering a particular activity, the entrepreneurs ensured that they were able to bring to the activity a better way of working or some inputs that would improve the efficiency of operations so that their entry would show positive results and would explicitly justify entry into a particular area.

The book provides learning opportunities for young women entrepreneurial aspirants who are concerned about striking a balance between their careers and their family lives and seek guidance from inspiring role models. It would also interest teachers of entrepreneurship and people involved in framing policies and running institutions that support women entrepreneurs. It would interest similar readers in other developing countries that have prejudices and sociocultural challenges similar to ours.

About the Author

Avinash Kirpal graduated from the University of Oxford in 1962 and then worked at the Tata Administrative Service for about 30 years at various positions including Public Affairs Officer for the Tata group in New Delhi, Corporate Planning Manager for Tata Exports Ltd and Vice-President of Tata International Ltd. Later, he became Secretary General of the World Federation of Trading Associations in Montréal.

During the last 10 years, he has been Advisor, Programmes for the Development of Small- and Medium-sized Enterprises at the International Management Institute (IMI), New Delhi, as well as Editor of IMI's quarterly magazine *Interface*. At IMI, he carried out several international consultancy assignments in the area of small enterprise development for the Word Bank, the International Finance Corporation, the United Nations Development Program, the International Trade Centre and the International Labour Organization.

His writings include *The SME and the Export Development Company*, published by the International Trade Centre, Geneva, and translated into French and Spanish, of which he is the co-author, as well as articles published in management journals and magazines.

His hobbies include travel—he has travelled to more than 60 countries for work and leisure—as well as watching old classic movies.